Marblehead Facts History & Old Photos

for Headers, Transplants & Tourists

By Dan Dixey

Copyright ©2025 by Dan Dixey

All rights reserved. This book or any portion thereof may not be reproduced or used in any manner whatsoever without the express written permission of the publisher except for the use of brief quotations in a book review.

Printed in the United States of America.

First printing, 2025

ISBN 978-0-9991074-4-7

Marblehead Images
8 Goose Pond Road
Acton, ME 04001

www.MarbleheadImages.com

In loving memory of
Adam B. Dixey
1979 - 2025

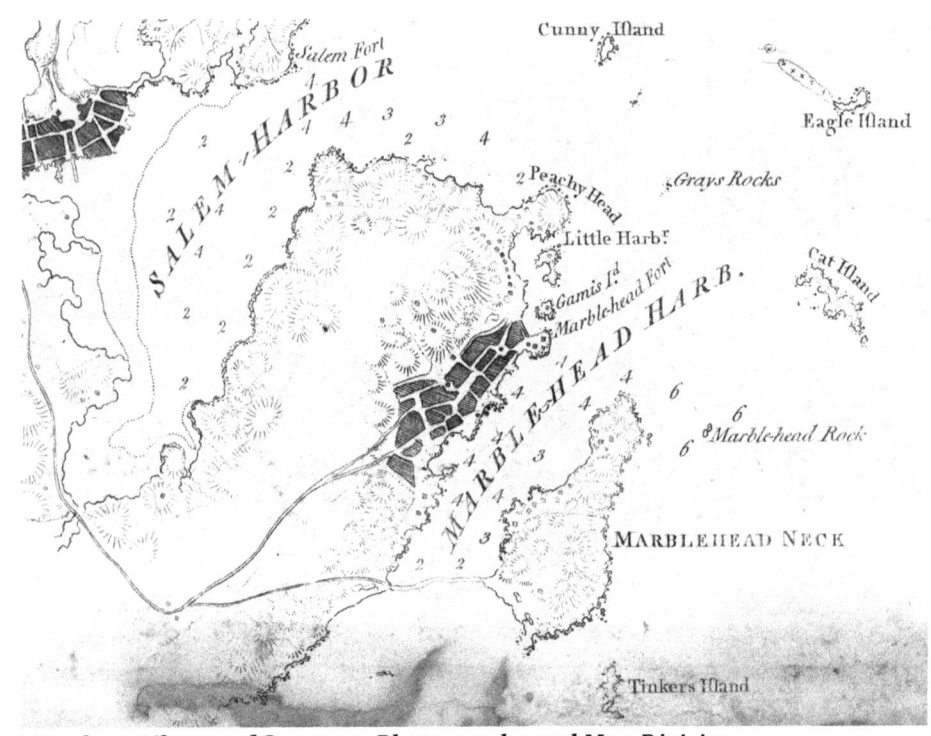
Map from Library of Congress, Photography and Map Division.

Preface

When people ask me where I am from, I get ready for the reaction to my answer. Marblehead is an affluent community with the reputation of being a snobby place. It's sad, but I have to laugh that so many people have no idea what the town was really like for about 340 years.

The town, when I was born, was still a fairly poor community. My grandparents lived on Nicholson Hill and had an outhouse and no bathroom in their house until the late 1950s. They never owned a car, but lived close enough to the railroad station to walk down and take a train for any travel out of town. When the Town-owned Veteran units were built at Barnard Hawkes Court, we were the first family to live in number 14. That is where we were living when I was born. It was a tight group of people who lived there. We knew all of our neighbors very well, and I am still friends with many of the kids who lived in the Court growing up. Marblehead was a quiet place where everyone knew you. It was full of history, and many of the families had ancestors who lived that history. When I hear the name Marblehead, that is the Town I remember, and want to remember.

Some of Marblehead's history will be explained in this book. Hopefully, you will acquire a better sense of what the town was like, and it will help you enjoy the history that surrounds you. It's impossible to include everything and everyone in one book, but this book should provide you with plenty of information. It will also spark questions that may lead you to additional research. It all helps to keep history alive.

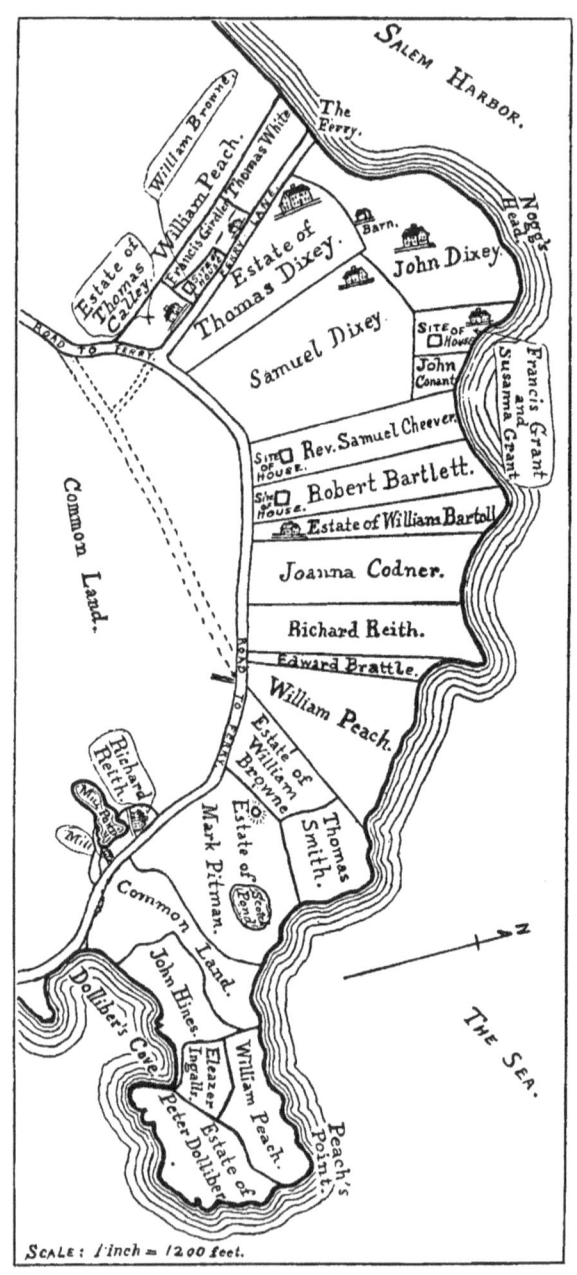

Map of Naugus Head to Peach's Point in 1700. Map by Sidney Perley.

1629

1629 was the year Marblehead was settled by English families. It was also the year that Reverend Francis Higginson referred to this rocky piece of uninhabited land as "Marble Harbor". In all probability, Higginson was standing in Salem and looking across Salem Harbor, and not Marblehead Harbor. The name has stuck for almost 400 years, so we will leave well enough alone!

1649

The wishes of the inhabitants finally came to fruition on May 2, 1649, when the General Court granted the petition allowing Marblehead to be incorporated as a separate town. Marblehead was always a thorn in Salem's side, so both towns were pleased with this ruling. The townspeople quickly gathered and selected their town leaders, also known as selectmen. Chosen were John Devereux, Moses Maverick, John Bartol, John Peach Sr., Samuel Doliber, Francis Johnson, and Nicholas Merritt.

1692 Witchcraft Hysteria

The height of the witchcraft hysteria peaked in Salem in 1692. This had people analyzing any peculiar behavior they could find with their neighbors. One such suspect resident of Marblehead, identified as Wilmot Redd, lived near the pond at the base of the hill of the meeting house and burial ground. She was also known as Wilmot Reed and was believed to have been married to fisherman Samuel Reed. Nicknamed Mammy Redd, she was always thought to have some unnatural powers, and rumors were constantly spread around town about her evil ways. An official complaint was filed against her on May 26, 1692, by several girls, claiming she inflicted pain upon them. A couple of witnesses from town testified that they saw her inflict a "stomach ailment" on one woman who was visiting Marblehead. The witnesses, Charity Pitman and Ambrose Gale, lived around the corner on Franklin Street. Mammy's trial took place in September, after being held in jail since her arrest in May. She was found guilty on September 17th and sentenced to be hanged on Gallows Hill. On September 22, the hanging took place, and Mammy and seven other women were hanged to their deaths. Several resolutions were passed, years after the convictions, clearing the names of many of the women. In 1998, a memorial stone was placed at Old Burial Hill for Mammy Redd. It wasn't until October 2001 that Mammy's name was officially cleared of any wrongdoing. Redd's Pond was named after the Wilmot "Mammy" Redd family.

1846 Gale

1846 was a tragic year for the Marblehead fishermen and the Town. Most of the fishermen only made one trip to the Grand Banks, off Newfoundland, that year. That was a journey that could take two weeks to complete, sailing from Marblehead Harbor. Ships sailed out on various dates, but a majority left Marblehead at the end of August and early September. Departing on August 27 were: the Schooner Trio under Skipper William Bridgeo, the Schooner Pacific with Skipper John Cross, the Schooner Liberty with Skipper Ebenezer Lecraw, and the Schooner Minerva with Skipper Francis Stephens On August 31, sailing were: the Schooner James Mugford under Skipper Richard Dixey, the Schooner Senator with Skipper Charles Chadwick, the Schooner Clinton under Skipper John White, and the Schooner Warrior with Skipper Sans Standley 2nd. The Schooner Zela sailed on September 1st under Skipper William Hooper alongside the Schooner Atlantic with Skipper Edward Dixey. On September 3rd, another fleet sailed off, including the Schooner Sabine under Skipper Samuel Dodd, the Schooner Hezron with Skipper Samuel Blackler, the Schooner Rebecca with Skipper Thomas Pedrick, and the eighty-three-ton Schooner Benjamin Franklin, owned by George Knight, under twenty-three-year-old Skipper Richard Frost. Captain Frost, of the Benjamin Franklin, many years later, recounted their experience during the trip that year. He recalled it was moderate weather when they left Marblehead, and they arrived at the outer Grand Banks in twelve days. After a dull week of fishing, he noted that on Friday, September 18th, as the wind picked up, he spotted about forty fishing vessels, most of them from Marblehead. The next morning, at daylight, they began their work with a threatening sky. By noon, a storm was moving in with high winds, a heavy sea, and some fog. They prepared by closing the hatches and "setting the reefed foresail". Within a half hour, the foresail was torn to pieces, but they were holding well, and the fog was lifting. Visibility was about three miles, and Frost only spotted one other ship, and said, "We were drifting towards her". As they both fought the wind, Frost recalled, "We worked for a position to the leeward of her and pretty soon crossed her bows, not more than a couple of hundred yards of water between us. It was the Sabine of Marblehead. I plainly saw two of her crew holding by the rail and recognized an Odd Fellow signal made by one of them. Just then, our mainsail was blown loose, and all hands were called to secure it; the Sabine passed from our thoughts for the time. When looking for her again, she was nowhere in sight. Mr. Pedrick, one of our crew, was the last man to see her. He noticed that the peak of her foresail had dropped, and the probability is that her peak halyards parted, as no sane man would attempt to lower a sail in such a blow. When this accident happened, the Sabine probably shipped a sea which filled and sank her. At any rate, we were the last to see her. This was about two o'clock in the afternoon (September 19)." The storm worsened, and Captain Frost said that John Freeto, one of his crew, pointed off into the distance. What they saw was a "monster of a sea" about a mile in the distance. It extended as far as they could see. Frost estimated it was over six miles wide and was a solid wall of water. As the wave approached, the Franklin was lifted to a great height, and the ship rolled so that the mast touched the water. As the wall of water passed, the crew opened the hatch and saw the wave "pass to the leeward where it broke not above a half a mile from their ship". The captain said, "Nothing that ever floated could have withstood the fall and shock of such a sea". He believed it was a tidal wave they witnessed. As the day went on, the storm cleared out, and the Franklin had only sustained minor damage. Three days later, the Franklin spotted Captain Philip Graves and his Schooner Hope, which was disabled and a total wreck. They were able to get the crew off safely and took what they could salvage before setting the Hope on fire. The Hope had been at sea for four months and was headed home to Marblehead when the storm hit. The next day, they met up with the Huguenot who was headed to New York. The Huguenot's Captain took the crew from the Hope back to New York with them, as the Franklin was staying out and wouldn't be returning to Marblehead until November. The Huguenot arrived in New York on October 3rd with Captain Graves and his crew. They would be the first to get word back to Marblehead about the horrific news, still not knowing the extent of the loss from this fierce gale. Sixty-five men and boys from Marblehead were lost on that September 19, 1846, day. One hundred and fifty-five children would never see their fathers again, and forty-three women instantly became widows. Lost that day, on the Schooner Pacific: John Cross, Eleazer Leach, Edward Homan, John Hunt, Isaac Wadden, Robert Devereux, and John Bates. On the Liberty: Ebenezer Lecraw, John Lancey, Samuel Graves, George LeMaster, Thomas Doliber, Robert Blair, and Richard Goss. On the Sabine: Samuel Dodd, Joseph Homan, David Pierce, Edward H. Dixey, Benjamin Garney Jr., Nicholas Florence, and Henry Pitman. On the Senator: Charles Chadwick, Joseph Graves, John Gilbert, Edward Dixey Jr., Mark H. Giles, John Glover, and Elisha D. Pedrick. On the Zela: William Hooper, John White Jr., John D. Bowden, Samuel Blackler Jr., Thomas Caswell Jr., John Wallace, and Amos Humphrey. On the Minerva: Francis Stevens, Philip Trasher, Osmond C. Stacey, Archibald Sinclair, William Wooldredge, Michael Phillips, and Browno Aleanda. On the Salus: John Trefry, Thomas Pedrick, Benjamin Martin, William Girdler, Joseph Atkins, Frederick Donaldson Jr., and John Green. On the Warrior: Sans Standley Jr., Benjamin Dodd, Moses Peachy, Edward Humphrey, William Blackler, George Bridgeo, and Samuel Goodwin. On the Trio: William Bridgeo, Edward F. Trefry, John Roads, Joseph Bowden, John Curtis, William Harris, and James Eastland. On the Clinton: John White 3rd. and Nehemiah Stone. In Marblehead, the news spread quickly, and every family in the town was affected by this tragedy at sea. The town was in shock for a very long time.

1877 Fire

In the early morning hours of June 25, 1877, a fire started in a barn behind the Marblehead Hotel on Pleasant Street. It quickly spread to the hotel and across the Brick Pond Reservoir, cutting off the water supply there. The town's firefighting equipment and limited water supply were no match for this raging fire. Building after building, and house after house, were catching fire and burning down, and most of the townspeople watched helplessly. The fire worked its way down Pleasant Street, School Street, Sewall Street, Spring Street, and Essex Street, destroying everything, including many large shoe factories. When the fire was over, eighty buildings had been destroyed, including thirty houses. Some of the buildings lost were the Railroad Depot, the General Glover Fire House, the new Fire House on School Street, still under construction, the South Church, the Marblehead Hotel, and the Allerton Block housing shoe factories, stores, a restaurant, and the Marblehead Messenger. Also destroyed were the F. W. & I. M. Monroe shoe factory, the Rechabite Building, the W. C. Lefavour shoe factory, the W. C. Gregory Apothecary, the Wormstead and Woodfin shoe factory, and many other businesses and homes. The town was devastated, but it began rebuilding immediately. A new railroad station was built, as well as the large Rechabite and Allerton blocks. Within years, Pleasant Street was lined with shoe factories again.

Aftermath of June 1877 fire

1888 Fire

The town met another unimaginable disaster on Christmas night in 1888. A couple, returning home from a Christmas celebration at the almshouse, noticed flames in the Power building, on the corner of School and Pleasant Streets. Before any alarms could be signaled, there was an explosion, and the flames spread quickly to surrounding buildings. In a replay of the fire from eleven years earlier, the fire jumped from building to building, spreading through the entire area destroyed previously. By the time this fire was out, over fifty buildings had burned down. Again, the shoe factories were the hardest hit. The Allerton Block and railroad depot were again lost along with William

Aftermath of 1888 fire looking up Pleasant Street

Lefavour's shoe factory, T. T. Paine, Humphrey & Brothers, Munroe's factory, the Masonic Hall, the Engine House, Cropley's factory, Woodbury Brother's Shoe Factory, W. C. Gregory's building with his Pharmacy, Peach's Factory, Stevens' Factory, the Rialto building and many other businesses and homes. During the fire, buckets of water were hand-carried up to the Abbot Hall tower to keep wetting it down. Live sparks were showering the town and wetting down the roofs, saved many buildings. Some reservoirs went dry, as the town's equipment pumped all night. After this second fire, the town instituted a fire-limit regulation, forcing any multi-story buildings in this fire district to be built of non-combustible material. The new railroad depot was built of brick, the Rechabite Building was brick, the School Street Firehouse and hardware store next door were brick, and William Gregory's block was rebuilt with bricks.

Abbot Hall

Benjamin Abbot was born in a house on the corner of Front and Union Streets, in Marblehead, on September 9, 1795. He was the son of Benjamin Sr. and Marcy Martin Abbot. Benjamin died on September 29, 1872. In his will, Benjamin left almost $100,000 to the Town of Marblehead, his birthplace. His only request was that it be used for a building, to benefit the inhabitants of the town, and that his name be associated with the building. The town chose the town common land, at the top of Training Field Hill, as the site, and chose the name Abbot Hall for the brick building. In July 1876, the cornerstone was set in place, and construction was started. James J. H. Gregory donated a clock and bell for the tower, and the building was completed and dedicated on December 12, 1877. At an earlier meeting in 1877, the town voted to use $20,000 of the Abbot Fund for a reading room for the use of the inhabitants. The reading room was put in Abbot Hall and named the Abbot Library. Note the spelling, as there is only one "T" in Abbot. It is one of the most misspelled words in town.

Abby Mays

In 1929, Abby May opened a candy store at 1 Atlantic Avenue and called it Abby May Candy Shoppe, and ran the store alone until her son Chester Elliott Roundy Jr. came home from the US Navy Reserves in 1946. Abby May was Abby May Chapman and was married to Chester Elliott Roundy Senior. When her son joined the business, they remodeled the store and added homemade ice cream to the menu. They ran the store until 1960, when they sold it to Robert Cotter. Cotter kept the name Abby May's until 1965, when he changed it to Cotter's. Around this time, businesses in town were complaining about kids hanging around stores and street corners. Cotter took the opposite stance and installed a jukebox in his store to encourage the younger crowd to gather there. Cotter's stayed in business until 1968, and in 1969, the House of Pizza opened in that location.

Adam's House

In 1894, near the foot of Franklin Street, on Front Street, John T Adams and Stone opened their small restaurant with four tables and a seating capacity of sixteen people, and called it "Adams and Stone". John Thomas Adams was the son of John Adams and Sarah R. Knapp and was born in Marblehead on August 22, 1864. John married Cora E. G. Bassett on December 25, 1883. They had three children. Their son, Clinton Foss Adams, was born June 12, 1884. He married Ethel C Snow on June 21, 1905. By 1897, John T Adams took over the restaurant and renamed it Adams House. That year, an addition was put on the building, and it could now seat forty-eight customers. In 1900, more space was added to the building, and the capacity was now one hundred and forty-eight. A new building was put up in 1908 that could hold one hundred and sixty-eight patrons. The rapidly growing business prompted John Adams to purchase the Sergeant McDonald Restaurant building at the entrance to Fort Sewall in 1914. He called this building the Adam's House Annex, and with these additional one hundred and twenty seats, he could now handle almost three hundred customers between the two buildings. A large sign, made of lights and standing thirty inches high, was placed on the Annex facing the harbor. In 1923, another new building was put up, this time made of stucco, and this one could seat three hundred and twelve people. The business continued to flourish until 1929, when the Great Depression hit and the stock market crashed. The business never fully recovered from the depression, and by the early 1940s, it was closed for almost five years. In 1946, the restaurant re-

Adams House on Front Street in August 1938

opened under new management, Howard Johnson's Inc. The business shut its doors for good in 1963, after over sixty years, and the building was torn down. The current four-story apartment building was built on this picturesque site overlooking the harbor.

Allerton

One family that arrived on the Mayflower in 1620 was the Allertons. This very wealthy family included Isaac Allerton and his wife Mary Norris, along with their three children, Bartholomew, Remember, and Mary. Isaac's wife, Mary, did not survive the winter and died in February 1621. Isaac was elected as an assistant to Governor William Bradford that year, and he was very involved in the affairs of Plymouth for many years to come. In September 1631, Isaac Allerton was sailing in the White Angel at Marblehead for his fishing business, a venture Matthew Craddock was involved in. Craddock was the first governor of the Massachusetts Bay Company. Allerton built his fleet up to eight boats to engage in fishing off Marblehead and had his son-in-law, Moses Maverick, working for him. It's unclear where Allerton's permanent home was. He still owned property in Plymouth, Massachusetts, had property in Maine, and still traveled back to England for his transatlantic business trips. He was living in one of the earliest houses in Marblehead, owned by Matthew Craddock, when it had a fire and burned down in 1633. In March 1635, the court ordered Allerton's removal from Marblehead. His shady business practices were catching up with him, so in May, he transferred his property and business assets in Marblehead to his son-in-law, Moses Maverick, and left Massachusetts.

Animal Control

There are constant complaints around Marblehead today about pet dogs. Barking, being off-leash, or worse, the dreaded canine poop around town. We all know it is not the animal's fault; unfortunately, they have entitled owners. Animal complaints are nothing new to Marblehead. In 1640, several men, including Thomas Dixey, brought some neighbors on Naugus Head into court for not building fences.

There were crops damaged by stray farm animals on Dixey's land, and the court was to assess the damages. Pigs, cows, goats, horses, sheep, and other animals were often roaming the streets in the 1600s.

Arnould Gallery Plein Air Painters

Back in 2006, Yves Parent, a renowned French marine painter, invited some artists to Marblehead to paint around town. Parent had art hanging in the Arnould Gallery, so Gene Arnould was also involved. Most years since then, Arnould has gathered some top artists to come to town and continue this tradition of painting around Marblehead, rain or shine.

Arnould Gallery 111 Washington Street, 2025

Gene Arnould moved to Marblehead in 1971 and eventually bought the house at 33 Mechanic Street. The house was built in 1721 by Isaac Mansfield and was remodeled by the Harris brothers around 1810. Gene Arnould was getting ready to open the Arnould Gallery in 1978, on the first floor of this home. At the same time, George's Lunch closed at 80 Washington Street, and that storefront became vacant. Gene opened at 80 Washington Street, close to his home, and stayed in that location until January 1993. The Gallery moved to 111 Washington Street in 1993, the store's current location, in 2025. In 1990, Arnould turned the first floor of his home on Mechanic Street into a bed-and-breakfast, called Brimblecomb Hill. In the thirty years as a B&B, they have hosted guests from every continent. The most colorful guest they have hosted was Keith Richards of the Rolling Stones. Richards, his wife, and some friends from Connecticut stayed a couple of nights and were very well behaved. Before they left, Keith Richards signed the guest book with "Great Bed, Thanks," then he scrawled a great signature across the rest of the page.

Arts Festival

The Marblehead Arts Festival began in 1962. Since then, it has grown to a yearly festival with artists, performers, musicians, and other entertainers. Thanks to a large list of volunteers, the festival hosts many events and displays in the downtown area, usually around the Fourth of July holiday.

Bands

The 1960s brought out quite a few local musicians who organized and played in rock-and-roll bands. I was most familiar with Jack and the Spades since my oldest brother, Mike Dixey, was the lead guitarist. I went to many of their practices and any concerts that I was old enough to get into. Three members were from out of town in the group: Nick Mantagouras on saxophone, Jack Brooks on drums, and Charlie Natheous, the singer. Besides my brother Mike Dixey, the other Marblehead boys were Doug Hill on guitar and Ed Waliakas on bass guitar. In 1964, the band traveled to New York and played at the World's Fair. Locally, they played at the YMCA,

1960s local bands (cards from Mike Dixey collection)

Lynn Auditorium, Salem Armory, The North Shore Music Theater, and once at the Warwick Theater. They never missed a Battle of the Bands event on the North Shore.
Another Marblehead band was Scotty and the Henchmen. That group consisted of Scott Sumner, Mike Clough, Brian McNulty, Mike Hill, Dave Saltman, and Bob Turner.

Bank Square

In 1804, a group of men believed the town could support a bank, and they drew up incorporation papers. The paperwork was approved, and the Marblehead Bank was formed. The Bank approached Samuel Sewall, who at the time owned the Lee Mansion at 161 Washington Street, and purchased the building for five thousand dollars. The bank later became the Marblehead National Bank and lasted until 1904, when it liquidated.

Sidewalk marker

In March 1831, a new bank, Grand Bank, was incorporated, being named after the Marblehead fishermen's favorite cod fishing destination, off Newfoundland. The bank purchased a property at 2 Hooper Street and built a granite block building, with a slate roof and bars on the windows, for use by the bank. In 1864, they voted to become a national bank, and in early 1865, they began operating as the National Grand Bank.

In 1871, the Marblehead Savings Bank was formed and moved into the Lee Mansion, next to the Marblehead National Bank. They later moved a few doors down to 153 Washington Street. With the National Grand Bank across the street, this intersection of Hooper and Washington Streets became known as Bank Square.

Barnard Hawkes Court

The population of Marblehead had grown to 13,765 in 1950, so there was a boom in the construction of new buildings, many of them town-owned. The town completed the Veterans housing units at Barnard Hawkes Court, and the first tenants moved there in 1950. My parents, Vincent and Mary Dixey, and my three older siblings moved into 14 Barnard Hawkes Court at that time. Vincent was a very young veteran, having been in the army, stationed in Germany at age eighteen. Other families living there before 1952 were Russell, Woods, Roberts, James, Drayton, Gerbrac, Thorner, Flachbart, Keenan, Grant, Homan, Cash, Broughton, Cohen, Phillips, Lund, Bassett, Blackler, Stone, and Pappas.

Barn Moving at Redd's Pond

A big event, often talked about, was Linc Hawkes moving a barn across Redd's Pond in 1965. There are many photos of Linc, in his dory, paddling across the pond with a rope attached to the barn. I recently obtained the actual story from the Libbey family. The barn belonged to the Libbeys and was on their property on the far side of Redd's Pond. John Libbey and Bill Hawkes (Linc's brother) devised the plan to move the barn to the other side of the pond. An attempt to move it across the ice in winter failed. In warmer weather, on the day of the move, all of the equipment was put in place, and a winch was attached to the barn. Linc put his dory in the pond and pretended to row the barn across. It was entertaining for the crowd that had gathered, and Linc was mistakenly credited with the "big move".

Beaches

Devereux, Riverhead (also known as Back Beach), Grace Oliver's Beach, Gas House Beach, Bessom's Beach, Goldthwaite Beach, Porter's Beach, Fort Beach (also called Flat Rock Beach), Danger Beach, Homan's Beach, Preston Beach, Stramski's Beach, Goldthwait Beach, and others are scattered around Marblehead. If you want to find them, look for the ocean.

Bench

"The Bench" is located at the Old Town House, facing State Street. For many years, this has been a gathering place for locals. When the Police Station was in the basement of the Town House, you could keep track of the criminal activities from this bench. In the 1960s, it was called the "Hippie Bench". Once the police department moved to Gerry Street in 1961, "brown bagging it" on the bench was a little easier to get away with.

Birthplace of the American Navy

America's first Naval ship was the "Hannah" and was manned by Marbleheaders. Nicholas Broughton, a Marbleheader, was the com-

Bumper stickers don't lie.

mander. It was outfitted and departed from Beverly on September 5, 1775. Colonel John Glover also commissioned another four ships, mostly manned by Marbleheaders. The country now had a Navy to battle those pesky British ships.

Black Joe

Black Joe's Tavern

Joseph Brown purchased a section of a house on Gingerbread Hill, next to a pond, in 1793. He had come from Rhode Island after having served in the Revolutionary War in exchange for his freedom. Joseph Brown was a slave in Rhode Island for the Brown family, and one of the family members was drafted to serve in the Army. It was allowed to have a volunteer substitute for a drafted person, and the Brown family made a deal with Joseph, an agreement they honored after he served. Now being free, Joe moved to Marblehead, bought a piece of property, and started a very successful tavern, known as "Black Joe's Tavern". He married Lucretia Thomas in 1794, in Marblehead, and eventually they purchased the other section of the house on Gingerbread Hill. Lucretia was known for her great cooking and her famous Joe Frogger cookies. When Joe applied for his pension for his war service, he was originally denied because he was not the only Joseph Brown who served. He was able to prove his identity and his service time and collected his pension after submitting additional information. The house and pond still sit up on Gingerbread Hill in Marblehead.

Boardman's Bakery

In 1937, the old Boardman Bakery building in Market Square, at the Mugford Street corner, was torn down. The town was very upset to see this old historic building removed to make room for a gas station. Francis Boardman started this bakery before 1877 and ran a very successful business for a number of years. The owner in 1937 was Malcolm Bell, and the town pleaded with him to restore the property and save the building. Bell let the building sit in disrepair and invested no money into the property. A Gulf Station was built and opened by Orrel Hansen by the summer of 1937. Besides gasoline, Hansen also sold batteries, tires, and tubes for the tires.

Boat Builder / Sail Makers

Frederick "Ted" Hood was operating a sail-maker shop at 15 State Street as early as 1952. Hood was a yacht designer, sailor, and sail-maker. He later moved the business, Hood Sailmakers, to Little Harbor.
Floyd Talbot Soule was a very talented man in Marblehead who worked at Hood Sailmakers for a number of years. Besides his regular job, he did house painting, carpentry, and was a boat builder. Soule was a Merchant Marine at sixteen and became quite a sailor over the years. In 1952, he finished building the wooden schooner, Red Shoes, and after four years' work, launched it from Marblehead Yacht Yard. The thirty-foot topsail schooner had a gaff topsail and fisherman staysail, a salt channel built into the hull, and the masts were rigged with old-style deadeyes and lanyards.
Chamberlain Boat Builder: William H Chamberlain was a carpenter and boat builder at 14 Orne St. Chamberlain retired in 1936 after over 40 years. He was a former Bank's fisherman.

Broughton Road

The second Veterans Housing Project was completed off of Humphrey Street on Broughton Road in 1951, and the first fifty people moved into these brick apartments.

Burgess

The Burgess Boat Club was formed in 1894 and was on Goodwin's Court. The members merged with the Boston Yacht Club in 1902, when BYC opened their Marblehead clubhouse. In 1905, William Starling Burgess and A. Appleton Packard purchased some land from the Parker estate on Marblehead Harbor to open a yacht building shop. Burgess came from a well-known and successful yacht designing and building family and was the son of Edward Burgess of Boston. This land off Nashua Place (now named Redstone Lane) became home to Burgess and Packard Naval Architects and Engineers, with a branch office in Boston. The first boat built there was the Pontiac, for George Silsbee, and many championship racing crafts were built there soon after. By the fall of 1909, Packard had left the Burgess and Packard Company in Marblehead, and Starling Burgess renamed the company W. Starling Burgess Ltd. In the factory off Redstone Lane, Burgess built his first airplane and completed it early in 1910. The plane was taken to Chebacco Lake, in the towns of Essex and Hamilton, for its first test flight. Burgess was assisted by A. M. Herring and Norman Prince on this historic "first airplane flight in New England". This same year, Burgess teamed up with Greely S. Curtis and incorporated the Burgess Company and Curtis, Inc. It was the first licensed aircraft manufacturer in the country. In 1911, they signed a contract with the Wright Brothers to build planes using their registered patent without modifications. They paid a fee to the Wright Brothers for each plane they produced. In 1912, Burgess added pontoons to the aircraft he built, violating his contract, and by 1914, the contract was dissolved. The Company name changed several times, but Burgess remained involved in building aircraft. Once World War I started, production switched to planes for the army and flying boats for the US Navy.

Burgess seaplane in Marblehead Harbor

In 1916, with demand being very high, Burgess built a second, larger factory on Little Harbor at Gas House Beach. The company employed close to eight hundred people. Test flights were flown at various locations over the years, including Marblehead Harbor. On November 7, 1918, the Little Harbor plant caught fire and burned down. With the war ending and increased competition in the airplane business, Burgess never rebuilt and closed the company. While living in Marblehead, Starling and his wife Rosamund Tutor Burgess, had a daughter, Starling, who was born at a hospital in Boston. Later, she was given Rosamund's surname, and when she was christened, her name was changed to Natasha. Tasha Tudor, as her name had evolved to, moved around the country and was influenced by the many successful people she met. Tasha was very creative and became a successful illustrator and writer of over one hundred children's books.

Car Dealers

Marblehead had a few car dealerships over the years. In the 1930s, Marblehead Motor Company was a Ford dealer on Atlantic Avenue and on Pleasant Street. There was also Miller Ford, Peach's Pontiac, Ingall's Motors, and others.

CBYC

Cheap Bastard's Yacht Club was started by Ray Till and a bunch of other people around the mid-1960s, down by the State Street wharf. From a bench, they would give their advice to everyone, whether they wanted it or not! Later, Lynn Marine on Front Street started selling bumper stickers. Some of the members were: brothers Bud, Joe, and Harland Bowden, Marvin Turner, Gerald Smith, Bill Dennis, Bill and Rene Conly, and others.

Christmas Walk

In December 1971, a group of merchants in Marblehead decided to get together and stay open late, for a weekend, for Christmas shoppers. The Bide-A-Wee restaurant stayed open late and offered free coffee. They decided to call it, are you ready… "Christmas Walk in Old Town"! (see Old Town definition, later in this book) This year, 2025, will mark the 55th annual Christmas Walk.

Churches

Around 1638, a meeting house was built on the top of Old Burial Hill. William Walton came to Marblehead and would become Marblehead's first minister, preaching in this new meeting house. Walton was unordained, but served as a trusted preacher in Marblehead for thirty years.
Money was raised in 1714, and a new building was constructed on Summer Street for the Protestant Episcopal Church. The materials for the framing were shipped over from England, and this house of prayer would be named St. Michael's Church. On July 20, 1715, Reverend William Shaw arrived in town as the rector of this church.
The Old North Church built a new church building on Washington Street in 1824. The congregation first met on Old Burial Hill under William Walton. They later moved to the new meetinghouse on Franklin Street, although the church wasn't officially established until 1684.
A Baptist Church was built in 1831 and dedicated in 1832, at 17-19 Pleasant Street. This building was destroyed by fire on the night of February 5, 1867. The church was rebuilt in the same location. It is now home to the Grace Community Church.
A new Methodist Episcopal Church was built on Summer Street and dedicated on September 11, 1833. The congregation had been meeting for over thirty years in a crude building on the rocks, near Rockaway and Pleasant Streets. In 1917, the church changed its name to St. Stephen's Methodist Episcopal Church.
The new brick Saint Stephen's Church was built in 1958 on Cornell Road, and the first service was held there in December of that year. The old wooden church on Summer Street closed after one hundred and twenty-five years of church services, and is now apartments.
The Universalist Church was built on the corner of Watson and Pleasant Streets in 1836. The church dedication was held on March

1, 1837. This original structure was leveled by a fire in 1880. A new church building was built in the same location and was completed in 1881. In March 1932, the steeple was removed for safety reasons. In January 1939, the Gut N Feathers Club officially opened in the old Universalist Church building, having bought it in 1938.

The Third Congregational Church, or South Church, was founded in 1858 by a group that left the First Congregational Church, being unhappy with a change of ministers there. They built a new church building in 1860 at the intersection of Essex and School Streets. The church burned down in the big fire of 1877 and was never rebuilt.

The Catholics in Marblehead originally attended church services at St. Mary's Church in Salem. As the number of parishioners grew, it was decided that Marblehead should have its own house of worship. By the late 1850s, a small church building was erected at the intersection of Prospect and Rowland Streets, and twenty years later, it was decided to build a new, larger church. The site chosen was Gregory Street, near Redstone Lane, where a rectory was built, and construction of a new church building began. In 1872, the new church, Star of the Sea, was just about completed on Gregory Street when a suspicious fire started in the building overnight. The building was destroyed in the fire, and although there was a strong suspicion that an unhappy neighbor may have been responsible for the fire, the cause of the fire was never officially determined. The parish, fearing the same thing would happen again, rebuilt a new church, back at the Prospect and Rowland Street site. A beautiful new church edifice was completed and dedicated in 1875, and served the parish for over fifty years. The seating capacity of three hundred was no longer adequate for the number of parishioners, so they decided to build a new stone church on the lower grounds of the church property. The ground was broken for the new seven-hundred-and-fifty-seat church on Atlantic Avenue in April 1928. The formal dedication of the new Star of the Sea Church was in July 1929, with over one thousand people showing up. The old wooden church building, up on the hill behind the new church, was taken down in 1930.

In November 1958, Temple Emanu-El broke ground on a new temple being built on Atlantic Avenue between Ames Road and Clifton

Avenue.

Temple Sinai purchased land from the Jewish Community Center of Greater Lynn on April 24, 1960, on Community Road in Marblehead and built a new temple, which opened in 1961.

In 1910, the Unitarian Church at 28 Mugford Street burned to the ground. A new church building was constructed on the same site. Today is known as the Unitarian Universalist Church.

The new Clifton Lutheran Church was completed in 1954 on Humphrey Street, between Hereford and Leicester Roads. Groundbreaking was in September 1953. Founded in 1941, the old combined church, parsonage, and parish hall were no longer adequate for the five hundred parishioners.

The Jewish Community Center of Greater Lynn was issued a permit on June 1, 1959, for the construction of the first building of a new facility on a thirteen-acre parcel off Atlantic Avenue in Marblehead. The project included indoor and outdoor recreational facilities.

Churn

The Churn on Marblehead Neck, near Castle Rock.

An attraction on Marblehead Neck that drew the attention of visitors and locals was the Churn. On private property, and visible from Castle Rock, this crevice in the rocks along the shore would shoot water high in the air. The rougher the sea, the higher the spray. One property owner removed some of the rocky ledge, and the formation today is hard to locate.

Clifton

In 1884, the residents of the Clifton section of town attempted to split off from Marblehead and form a separate "Clifton Village". This plan was rejected by the town. The Clifton area was built up by Benjamin Ware when he opened the Clifton House hotel in 1846, on farm land the family owned. In 1847, Ware married Hannah Clifton, from Salem, and the hotel, and subsequently, the entire area got the name Clifton, from that family connection. In the 1870s, the new railroad line and train stop in Clifton were a big boost to the hotel business.

Sailors at Clfton in 1918

Cook's Corner

Cook's Corner is the intersection of Washington Street and Pleasant Street, at the lower end. The Grader Block is the building on the corner, where the Mud Puddle toy store is today. As early as 1903 and as late as 1940, that corner store at 1 Pleasant Street was occupied by Richard M. Cook, a jeweler.

Cresap

The town hired a consulting firm in 1989 to assess and make recommendations on ways to save money on the operating expenses of the Town of Marblehead. The Cresap Report was produced and became one of the biggest argument subjects in town. Major cutbacks were recommended, and many didn't believe these cuts were in the best interest of the town, especially the department heads who were asked to slash their departments. The study, which cost the town $65,000, recommended laying off over fifty-four of the Marblehead town employees. Recommendations were to cut fifteen police, ten fire, eighteen school department positions, and others.

Damon Tucker's

Arthur Damon Tucker opened a radio and camera store, A. Damon Tucker, and was at Essex and Washington Streets in 1940. He moved the store to 25 Atlantic Avenue and was called Damon Tucker's, selling hobbies, records, televisions, and more. A British invasion hit the United States in the 1960s, but this time it wasn't necessary to man the forts. British rock and roll groups were taking over the top ten charts with their music, and Damon Tucker's Store was the place to go. I bought my first 45 RPM record, by The Beatles, at Damon Tucker's for under a dollar. It was recorded in England by Capitol Records and had "I Want to Hold Your Hand" on one side and "I Saw Her Standing There" on the flip side. The store was also the place to buy plastic model car kits and other hobby kits for kids. Damon and his wife Eleanor ran the store for many years. The store closed in December 1968.

Deed

On August 15, 1672, Ahawton, Native Indian Ruler of Natick, stated under oath in court that he knew "George with No Nose" was once the sagamore of Marblehead's land. According to their custom, that would make him the owner of Marblehead. George passed this ownership on to James Quanapohkowmet but kept a one-half interest in the land. Since the colonists' land ownership in New England was based on the Massachusetts Bay Colony Charter, most towns were looking to get actual deeds of ownership. Marblehead did not believe any claims of ownership to be valid, but in 1684, a committee was appointed to resolve any issues. The committee was composed of: John Devereux, a fisherman; Moses Maverick, a merchant; Samuel Ward, a cooper; Thaddeus Riddan, a merchant; William Beal, Richard Reed, a fisherman; Nathaniel Walton, and Thomas Pitman. Devereux and Ward were authorized to settle any claims. They came to an agreement with James and paid him fourteen pounds and thirteen shillings to release the land claim. On July 18, 1684, a deed was prepared and signed, and an addendum was later signed by Joseph Quanapohkownat, also called Joseph English, who was mentioned in the original deed. This has now removed any doubt about the rightful ownership of the town. Marblehead was unoccupied, with no permanent structures, when the English families settled here in the late 1620s. Claims that anyone was "displaced" or that "land was stolen" are completely inaccurate and not factual pertaining to Marblehead. Other parts of New England may have had completely different circumstances when they were settled.

Desire

In 1636, a one-hundred-and-twenty-ton ship, the Desire, was built in Marblehead. The exact location is unknown, but most likely in the Barnegat section, near Little Harbor. The ship was built for Captain William Pierce of Boston, one of the most experienced sea captains in the area. The Desire was constructed as a commerce ship to be used in the very busy trans-Atlantic trade business, but became known as the first ship used in the colonies to transport slaves. On one return trip in 1638, the ship was loaded with "product and negro slaves" and brought back to New England. This slave trafficking was sadly a worldwide and accepted practice, but some leading citizens of Boston criticized this action by the New England ships. In 1641, the Massachusetts Body of Liberties was established in New England by the Massachusetts General Court. The code in Passage 91 legalized the owning of slaves and would remain in effect in Massachusetts until 1780.

Devereux, Jane

Jane Smith Devereux was the daughter of Samuel Devereux and Hannah W. Smith Devereux and was born on February 11, 1858, in Marblehead. She was the 5th great-granddaughter of John Devereux, one of Marblehead's first selectmen and owner of the three hundred and fifty-acre "Devereux Farm". She received her medical degree at Boston University in 1880 and was the town's first female physician and one of the only female doctors in the country. She never married and dedicated her entire life to caring for the residents of her hometown. In 1896, Dr. Jane Devereux started the Visiting

Nurses Association along with others, including Miss Mary Graves, Rev. S. Linton Bell, Mrs. Grace Oliver, Miss Mary A. Alley, and Miss Eleanor Goldthwait. Miss Lewis was hired as the first nurse and was paid twenty-five cents an hour, and walked her route daily. In 1915, Devereux was appointed school physician at the Roads School. By 1918, she was the first aid instructor for the local Girl Scout troop. In 1920, many of the town's physicians purchased automobiles to make their rounds, but Dr. Devereux kept her reliable horse-powered transportation. By the time the first winter ended, several of the other physicians went back to horse transportation, having too many problems learning how to get around on the snow-covered roads in Marblehead in a gasoline-powered vehicle. By late 1920, she gave in to the modern ways and purchased an automobile of her own and sold her horse "Lady". Her wagon driver for the previous thirty years was Edward Gorman, and he never took a vacation during that period. In 1923, Dr. Devereux was in an accident while pulling her automobile from her office driveway at 72 Pleasant Street on a Sunday morning. Her vehicle was hit by a trolley car, and she sustained a minor head injury. She was treated by another Marblehead physician, Dr Perley L. Sanborn. In 1934, Dr Jane Devereux was again appointed as a school physician, a position she had held for over thirty years. Other school physicians appointed were Dr. Perley Sanborn, Dr Edward Burbeck, Dr. Samuel Eveleth, and Dr. Franklin Ireson. The school nurse reappointed that year was Miss Ella Cortee. Dr. Jane Devereux retired on January 1, 1940, just shy of her 82nd birthday. Later that month, she was admitted to the Mary Alley Hospital for overexposure. Jane passed away on December 26, 1940, at the home of her niece, Mrs. Richard Sanders, on Atlantic Avenue. She was truly an amazing woman and lived her long life doing what she loved.

Devereux, John

John Devereux was born in Stoke-by-Nayland, Suffolk, England, in 1615. He was in the Salem and Marblehead area around 1630. When Marblehead incorporated as a Town, Devereux was elected as one of the first Board of Selectmen members in 1649. In 1659, Devereux purchased 350 acres of land along the sea almost to the Great Neck (Marblehead Neck). The area became the Devereux Farm. When a road was laid out to the Neck in 1670, it ran through the Devereux Farm. The area is still referred to as Devereux, and a street, a terrace, and a beach are named for this family.

Down Bucket

When you heard the shouting of "down bucket" from up above, you did not look up. This was a warning that a resident was dumping their chamber pot out of the window. Tucker Street, being a steep hill, received the nickname of "shittin hill"! The reply to "down bucket" would be "up for air".

Entitlement

There is a fair amount of entitlement in Marblehead today. Entitled is a title you get that allows you to park on crosswalks, park in front of driveways, double park, bypass lines at the school because you are more important than the rest of the people in line, drive like a maniac and tailgate those in front of you because YOU have someplace to be and on and on and on!

Entitlement: belief that one is deserving of or entitled to certain privileges. Synonym: asshole.

Jermyn Farm

The Jermyn Farm on Village Street was the last dairy farm in Marblehead, and it closed in 1958. It had been the Harris Farm previously. Henry Byors bought the property and built a new brick house in 1959 for his

Jermyn's Dairy Farm on Village Street.

family home at 55 Village Street. The Jermyn family kept a couple of lots from the parcel and moved their old house to one of those lots. Henry Byors had a barn behind the house with a few farm animals. In the very back of the property were fields and a swamp, and the property may have backed right up to the Robinson Farm. It was a great property for kids to explore, and between the Byors, the Wheelers, and the Dixeys, there were plenty of kids around that neighborhood in the 1960s.

Ferry

Marblehead had many different ferry boats operating, both in Marblehead Harbor and on the west shore. The earliest ferry ran from Naugus Head to Salem and was run for many years by Thomas Dixey, starting in 1644. Some more recent ferry boats, in Marblehead Harbor there were: Blonde, Delta, Queen, Kelpie, Brunette, and others.

Fire Department

The Fire Department was organized in Marblehead in 1751. Robert Hooper Esq., a wealthy resident, purchased a fire engine and presented it to the town as a gift. The town graciously accepted the apparatus and voted on a Board of Firewards. They were: Nathan Bowen, Robert Hooper, Richard Reed, George Newmarsh, and Jeremiah Lee. The Moses Allen Pickett Fire Association was formed in 1866. The Marblehead Steam Fire Association was formed in 1872. In 1877, the town's fire apparatus consisted of the Steam Fire Engine on Pleasant Street, the M. A. Pickett on Franklin Street, the General Glover Engine on Pleasant at the Brick Pond Reservoir, the Mugford Engine at 163 Washington Street, the Gerry Engine on State Street, the Liberty Hose at the Town House in Market Square, and the Washington Hook and Ladder at Washington and Middle Streets. The new School Street firehouse was put into use after being rebuilt after the big 1877 fire. In 1880, the Mugford Building was built at 112 Washington Street and was occupied by the Mugford Fire Association.
A site was selected for a new fire station on the corner of Pleasant Street and Ocean Avenue, and $154,600 was appropriated for the

project. In 1958, James "Chummy" Frost, of Marblehead Salvage Company, removed the old Goldthwait house from the property. The new station was dedicated and opened in 1959 under the leadership of Fire Chief John Adams. Now, all of the Town's fire apparatus operated out of this new station and the Franklin Street Station.

In 1999, the Board of Selectmen unanimously voted to sell the old Marblehead Fire Station property, at 12 School Street, to the Marblehead Little Theatre.

Fishing

Hard-working fishermen and their families built Marblehead. Today, Marblehead still has a good number of men and women engaged in fishing and lobster fishing. A whole book could be written on this subject. In 2023, I made a documentary titled "Lobster Fishing in Marblehead". It is a 2-hour film, highlighting many of the people involved in this trade over the years.

Floyd Ireson

In 1779, Captain Ephraim Ireson purchased the house at 19 Circle Street. Ephraim's daughter, Miriam, inherited the house and in 1802, sold the top floor to her uncle, Captain Benjamin Ireson, nicknamed Floyd. In October 1808, Captain Benjamin Ireson and his crew set out on one of their typical fishing trips aboard Ireson's ship, the Betty. On the return trip, during a bit of a storm, they came across another vessel off Cape Cod. This schooner, the Active, put out a call for help. Ireson discussed with his crew their options for offering help. The crew wanted to return to Marblehead and avoid any risk during this storm. Ireson suggested dropping anchor and waiting out the storm, but was met with vehement opposition from the crew. They returned to Marblehead without stopping. The next day, another passing ship rendered help but could only save a few of the crew on the Active. Back in Marblehead, the crew spread a story that Captain Ireson refused to stop or help the sinking schooner. Marblehead was outraged by what they were told, and the story was confirmed by surviving crew members from the Active when they returned to port. Being a town full of fishermen and sea captains, who all support each other when needed, the residents were furious about the actions of Ireson. Not knowing the facts, some men and boys in town took matters into their own hands to see that Ireson was punished. They tarred and feathered Ireson and paraded him around town in a wagon. The parade could not enter Salem, so the group turned around and eventually dumped Benjamin Ireson back in town. Captain Ireson remained calm during the entire ordeal and only spoke once, telling his kidnappers that "they would regret their actions". Eventually, the truth came out, but the story blaming old Floyd Ireson never stopped being told.

Forts

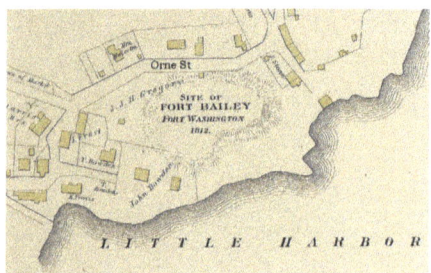
1888 Map Section

Soon after the English settlers had arrived in 1629, a fort was built on the tip of Naugus Head and was called Darby Fort. A large ordinance, or cannon, was sailed over from England and placed in the fort. Marblehead was often referred to as the Darby Fort side of Salem. In later years, this fort was manned and called Fort Miller. Fort Sewall: No, it's not pronounced Sea wall, and it is not spelled Sewell. It's Sewall and pronounced Soowill, or if you're local, just Sool. Fort Sool. The court, in 1644, appointed a constable, David Curwithin, to watch over the residents of Marblehead and also directed the town to fortify its shore. In response, a fort was established on the head of land, at Marblehead Harbor, called Gale's Head. Renovations were done to Gale's Head Fort from 1798 to 1801. After the work was completed, the Fort was renamed Fort Sewall, after Chief Justice Samuel Sewall. Sewall was born in Boston on December 11, 1757, and married Abigail Devereux in 1781. They were living in Marblehead before 1790.

Tensions between the Northern States, loyal to the Union, and the Southern States, which separated into the Confederate States, came to a head in 1861, with the start of the Civil War. President Lincoln called for troops on April 15, 1861, and the next day, Marbleheaders were in Boston and were the first groups to arrive. Most of the Marblehead men were in Company B, C, and H of the Eighth Regiment Massachusetts Volunteer Infantry. During the War, Marblehead outfitted Fort Miller on the site of the old Darby Fort, on Naugus Head, manned Fort Glover (previously called Cow Fort), at the top of what is now Bubier Road, and the hill behind Seaside Park, and did some needed repairs to Fort Sewall.

Fountain Park is located on Orne Street, across from the Old Burial Hill entrance. It was once named Bailey's Head and was the location of a fort during the Revolutionary War. During the War of 1812, it was called Fort Washington. The land was donated to the Town by James J.H. Gregory in 1888.

Fred Litchman

Frederic Brigham Litchman was born August 26, 1869, in Marblehead and was the son of William Litchman and Sarah E. Bartlett. He married Coralie Mason on November 12, 1902, in Marblehead. Coralie was born on November 2, 1875, in Marblehead and was the daughter of Isaac Wyman Mason and Lydia A. Dennis. Fred Litchman started Litchman's Photography and Printing Company in 1898 and was at 15 State Street, sharing a building with the Marblehead Laundry (Maddie's Sail Loft is now in that location). In 1914, Litchman moved his photography business to 157 Washington Street, next to the Lee Mansion. Fred and his wife Coralie moved into the top-floor apartment above the photography studio. Litchman captured Marblehead life in his photographs from 1898 through the 1930s and was the most important photographer in town during that period.

Gangs

Neighborhood kids often stuck together as groups around Town. They would be referred to by the neighborhood they came from. There were Wharf Rats, Reeds Hillers, Barnegaters, Shipyarders, and others. For entertainment, they would have rock fights, and they developed good throwing arms and accuracy. The term

"Rockem" was used for this activity.

Gas Stations

Today, no public gas stations exist in Marblehead. There have been over 25 gas stations in Marblehead over the years. At one time, you could stand in the middle of Atlantic Ave, in front of where Shubie's is today, and see 7 gas stations. (I don't suggest you ever stand in the middle of Atlantic Ave today.) There was: Frost's Shell Station on the corner of Atlantic Ave and Washington Street, Phil's Mobil (the last station in town), Texaco Station where Shubie's Marketplace is, Charlie Lee's Gulf Station, an Esso Station where Mino's is, a station where West Marine is, and a gas station where the plaza between Commercial and Central Streets sits. Coca-Cola would occasionally run promotions and put puzzle pieces in the bottle caps of soda bottles. My brother, Barry, and I would ride our bikes around town and ask for all of the bottle caps from the Coke machines at each gas station. My mother must have loved it when we came home with a brown paper bag full of sticky bottle caps and dumped them on the kitchen table to sort them!

Glover's Marblehead Regiment

On January 10, 1775, Marblehead held a Town Meeting and voted for a pay schedule for those who would become minutemen and train in "the art of war". The intent was to build a strong militia and be prepared to defend the province and protect the rights of the entire country. This Marblehead group would end up playing a key role in the Revolution. Colonel John Glover would lead the men, and by June 1775, the gathered companies had grown to over 400 men. On June 21, 1775, Glover and his men received orders to march to Cambridge to join the Provincial Army. The next day, the regiment and the following officers arrived in Cambridge: Colonel John Glover, Lieutenant Colonel John Gerry, Major Gabriel Johonet, Adjutant William Gibbs, Captains William R. Lee, William Courtis, William Bacon, Thomas Grant, Joel Smith, Nicholson Broughton, William Blackler, John Merritt, John Selman, and Francis Symonds. Lieutenants John Glover Jr., Robert Harris, William Mills, William Bubier, John Bray, John Stacey, Nathaniel Clark, Joshua Prentiss, Isaac Collyer, and William Russell. Ensigns Edward Archbold, Thomas Courtis, Seward Lee, Ebenezer Graves, Joshua Orne, John Devereux Jr., Nathaniel Pearce, Robert Nimblett, Edward Homan, and George Sinecross. Privates in the ten Companies included familiar names in Marblehead history such as Bartlett, Bowden, Cash, Caswell, Dixey, Doliber, Frost, Girdler, Getchell, Goodwin, Hawley, Hooper, Humphrey, Martin, Mason, Orne, Peach, Pedrick, Pickett, Ramsdell, Russell, Selman, Snow, Stacey, Trefry, Tucker, Williams, Vickery and many others. Glover's crew impressed the higher officials. Their sailing skills and experience on the sea led General Washington to authorize them to prepare vessels, to patrol the coastline down to Boston. They set up in Beverly and on September 5, 1775, Captain Nicholson (also called Nicholas) Broughton and men from the Regiment sailed out on the schooner Hannah. This new Navy was very successful in capturing British ships and their precious cargo of weapons and ammunition. The Army was reorganized on January 1, 1776, and most of the same men from the Twenty-first Regiment re-joined and became the Fourteenth Continental Regiment. This very diverse group was led by Colonel John Glover, Lieutenant Colonel Gabriel Johonet, and Major William R. Lee. On July 20, 1776, Glover's Regiment left Beverly for New York, arriving on August 9th. The Regiment was successful in many missions, but their biggest and most important job came on the night of December 25, 1776. Glover and his men took General George Washington, Commander-in-Chief of the Continental Army, along with his army and supplies, and crossed the Delaware River into Trenton, New Jersey. The weather was stormy and cold, and the Hessian-maned Garrison was not prepared for the attack that took place in the early morning hours. The victory in this battle was one of the biggest turning points of the Revolution. Washington's weakened army was at a low point, and this important win boosted morale and brought in large numbers of new enlistments. Many historians believe the Revolution may have been lost if not for this key military maneuver.

Today, you may come across the Glover's Regiment reenactment group around town, in period clothing, at various events. You may hear them marching to the beat of a drum and, if you're lucky, hear the firing of the old black powder muskets and blunderbusses.

Graves Boat Yard

In 1933, the Graves Yacht Yard purchased the Stearns & McKay Yacht Yard property at 89 Front Street on Marblehead Harbor, next to Dixey's Wharf. Stearns had a boatyard and railway as early as 1895 in that location. It later became Stearns & McKay. Graves Yard was started by James Elbridge Graves at his property on Little Harbor in the early 1900s and was later joined by his children, James Jr. and Edith. Graves bought the old Glover Inn building across Front Street and had it moved to the waterfront in 1936 by Frank Goodwin and his crew. The building had to be moved and turned ninety degrees to set it along the harbor, where it still sits today.

Great Race

"The Great Race" was not the slogan of a local white supremacy group! Actually, some Marbleheaders were sitting in Maddie's, on State Street, one night in 1968, and a discussion came up about racing from Boston to Marblehead and if it could be done faster by land or by sea. A challenge was set up, and the very first Great Race from Watertown to Marblehead was held that summer. The rules were that no motors or engines could be used, and you could go by land or sea.

Sign on the wall at Maddie's Sail Loft

There was an entry fee that covered a t-shirt, and there were drinks at the finish line on State Street at Maddie's. The race grew, and the neighbors didn't appreciate this event, so the finish line was moved to Devereux Beach in subsequent years. People were building multi-person bikes and boats, and some groups came up with costumes to wear during the race. If you won the race, it was assumed you cheated, and you were disqualified, and the same applied to finishing second or third or finishing at all, so no official winner was really declared. Kegs of beer

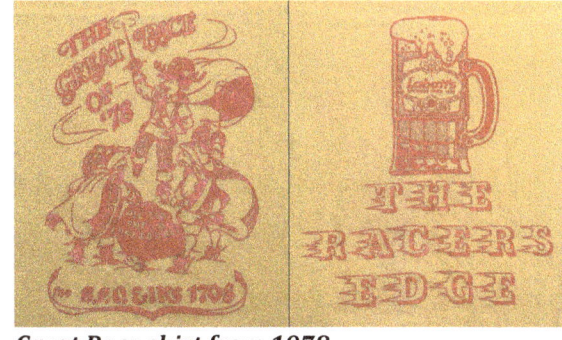

Great Race shirt from 1978

were waiting for the racers when they arrived at the beach, and a good time was had by all. Well, okay, not all the townspeople appreciated this top-notch athletic event. In 1978, the Town of Marblehead would not approve the use of Devereux Beach, so the finish line was eventually moved to Nahant. Many people fought hard to get this race back to Marblehead, to no avail. Eventually, the MDC refused to allow the Nahant location for the finish line, and the Great Race, as we knew it, came to an end.

Grocers

In the 1950s and 1960s, the First National grocery store was located at 123 Pleasant Street and was just one of many grocery stores scattered around Marblehead. In 1961, they started giving out S & H Green Stamps. The biggest thing I remember

First National Stores on Pleasant Street next to the Warwick Theater circa 1940

about the store was the smell of fresh coffee beans as soon as you walked in the door. They kept the beans and a grinder on the left wall as you entered the store. The store closed in 1968.

As early as 1933, Louis Shube ran a grocery store at 44 Atlantic Avenue, and Daniel J. Colbert ran a grocery store across the street, at 41 Atlantic Avenue. Shube's Grocery Store moved across the street to 45

Atlantic Avenue and was later run by Louis' daughter, Esther Shube Habin, and her husband, Dave. Lastly, Shube's grocery store was run by their son, Lawrence Habin, still at 45 Atlantic Avenue. This is the current location of CVS Pharmacy in 2025. Colbert's Store had a liquor license, which Bill Shube purchased in 1948. Bill Shube ran the Liquor Store in the building connected to Shube's Grocery Store, but it was a separate business. The current Shubie's store at 16 Atlantic Avenue is a direct descendant of Colbert's Liquor Store, which was owned by Bill Shube and is now run by Bill's son, George, and his family.

Frank Norris Osborne started a small grocery and meat market at 28 South Street in 1911. In 1913, with partners, he bought the Goss Grocery business and moved into that building on School and Pleasant Streets. Osborne bought the building from Goss in 1919 and continued the grocery store, FN Osbornes, for many years. It was a true family business, and many Marbleheaders worked in the store over the years. There was a liquor store in the front of the building, on the Pleasant Street side. Later, sons Charles, Frank Jr., and Bowden were running the store, then Charles retired in 1974. Frank Jr. was the last Osborne to run the store. The grocery store closed in the 1980s, and the liquor store closed about ten years later.

Around 1912, Ed Haley opened a grocery store, Haley's Public Market, at 105 Washington Street. Haley died in December 1931, and Charlie Kelley, a cousin of Haley's wife, took over the grocery store. In the 1930s, he obtained a liquor license. In 1944, Kelley purchased the Mugford Building across the street and moved his grocery store, with a liquor license, into the first floor. Another grocery store, run by Louie Halpert and Buck Lawton down the street, approached Kelley in 1953 about moving his business into the Mugford Building. They struck a deal, and Louie's Marblehead Supermarket ran a grocery store, and Kelley kept his liquor license and ran a separate liquor store next to the grocery store. Lawton sold his half of the business to Halpert in 1968. Charlie Kelley's son, John, worked in Haley's Liquor Store, and when Charlie died in 1982, John took over the store. In 1983, when Marblehead Supermarket closed, Kelley renovated the building, restoring its original look. Haley's Wine and Spirits is still at

114 Washington Street in the Mugford Building.

Penni's Market was at 118 Washington Street and was opened by Samuel and Frances Penni in 1931, originally as a fruit store. Penni's was another family-run grocery store employing many Marbleheaders. The store was sold to sons, Joseph and Daniel (known as Bill), in 1957. Joseph sold out to Bill in 1973. Their sister Theresa was with the business for fifty years, and their brother Al also worked in the store. The supermarket was sold to Jim Crosby in 1989. A large fire on September 5, 1994, burned down the original building. Occasionally, some pranksters would remove one of the letters "N" from the sign.

Gun House

In 1808, the town agreed to build a brick gun-house on the southerly side of the Workhouse lot, on what became Back Street, and is now named Elm Street. The building was not used for long as an armory, but it is still standing.

Gun House on Back Street (now Elm)

Halifax Race

The first Marblehead to Halifax Race took place in 1905. It was coordinated by the Eastern Yacht Club, and six schooners took part in that first, 360-nautical-mile yacht race. The race became more formalized in 1939 when the Boston Yacht Club was involved, and it became an every-other-year event.

Headers

Okay, let's talk about the touchy subject of defining a Header! Anyone who lives in Marblehead, as a resident, is a "Marbleheader". But, what is a "Header"? Many different rules have been thrown around over the years, but here is what I will offer. You are a real "Header" when others refer to you as one, not because you call yourself one.

It doesn't matter where you were born, or how many generations of your family were born in Marblehead. It's a title you have to earn. The definition of Transplant is obvious. Anyone who moves to Marblehead from elsewhere is a transplant. But, you can be a transplant AND a Header, if you earn the title. Now, the easiest one to define is a "True Header". If you were born in Marblehead in the Mary Alley Hospital, or at home, or in the grandstands at Seaside Park, or anyplace else in Marblehead, you are a True Header. No discussion or arguments about this one, just check your birth certificate if you are not sure. Now, what does all of this mean? Absolutely nothing, but that won't stop people from arguing about it.

Herreshoff

Lewis Francis Herreshoff was born on November 11, 1890, in Bristol, Rhode Island. He was the son of Nathaniel Greene Herreshoff and Clara Anna DeWolf. Nathaniel was a famous yacht designer, and his son followed the family trade. L. Francis Herreshoff purchased the castle at Crocker Park in 1945 and made it his home and studio. Herreshoff believed wood was the only material that should be used in yachts. Besides yachts, he also designed many small crafts from his Marblehead studio. He was often seen in Marblehead Harbor rowing one of the kayaks from his own design. Herreshoff died in December 1972.

Hollyhocks

Hollyhocks on Front Street

The unofficial "Marblehead flower" is the Hollyhock. Once lining most streets in Town, the Hollyhocks seemed to grow in any crack or crevice, but are now hard to find around town.

Honey Wagon

"Honey Wagon' was the nice name for the cesspool-pumping trucks that used to do their job around town. Not a pleasant odor when the truck was near.

BF Martin Jr, honey wagon at Green Street and Lincoln Ave.

Hooper Mansion

The King Hooper Mansion, 8 Hooper Street, was built in 1728. In 1888, the YMCA purchased the King Hooper Mansion and moved there from Lyceum Hall. The Marblehead Arts Association bought the King Hooper Mansion in 1938 and still occupies the building today.

Hotels

In 1882, the large Nanepashemet Hotel was built for Robert Bridge on Marblehead Neck, overlooking the Atlantic Ocean, at the east end of Nanepashemet Street. The wrap-around balcony allowed for full viewing of yacht races from start to finish. The hotel had sixty-five rooms for guests, each one connected to the main office by an electric bell. The building was lit by gas lamps, and the gas was manufactured by an on-site machine, in the ground behind the hotel. A pond provided fresh water, with a windmill powering a pump that delivered the water to a tank on the roof. As tourism was increasing, this was a much-needed hotel on the neck. Previously, there were limited rooms in some small boarding houses, and most of the summer cottages were privately owned and used by the owners.

Nanepashemet Hotel on Marblehead Neck, built in 1882

A big fire burned down the fifty-room Crowninshield Hotel on Clifton Avenue in 1913. The hotel had been owned by Samuel Hobbs since 1903 and was one of the older hotels, dating back to pre-1890. The Clifton House was a hotel built in 1846, on Clifton Avenue, by Benjamin P. Ware, with help from his father, Erastus Ware. One of the earliest boarding houses in the area was that of Erastus Ware, at the house on his farm in Clifton. In 1893, the Clifton House hotel building was destroyed by fire.

As early as 1888, Mrs. G. A. Brackett owned cottages on the second cove, on a piece of land known as Skinner's Head, or Rockmere Point. This property was accessible from Gregory Street. These cottages were rented out to visitors, usually for the entire summer, and proved to be a great vacation spot for families. In 1901, a new, one-hundred-room hotel was built on this land by the Brackett family and named the Rockmere Hotel. Overlooking Marblehead Harbor, this hotel was a very popular destination for many years. In May 1930, a fourteen-thousand-pound anchor was brought down from Maine and moved to the property by Woodfin Brothers' moving company. The anchor was placed on Gregory Street and was used to hang the hotel's sign. In 1937, the hotel was sold and was re-named Hotel Marblehead, though the locals continued to call it The Rockmere. The hotel was sold again in 1941, and by 1958, it housed the Quarterdeck Yacht Club. In 1963, the building was closed up and sat empty until it was torn down in 1965. The Glover Landing condominiums were built there in 1966. Only the anchor remains now, on Gregory Street. There was also the Atlantic House on Washington Street and The Leslie on Front Street.

Howards

Howard's News and Stationery store was located at 112 Pleasant Street, on the corner of School Street. It was there as early as the 1930s and was a very busy newspaper store in its day. We bought all of our baseball cards there, and of course, our Mad Magazines, featuring Alfred E. Neuman! There is a pet store there now.

Hutchie's

In 1890, Theodore Hutchinson opened his store, Hutchinson Potato Chip Company, at 151 Pleasant Street, featuring his home-made chips. Theodore's son, Samuel, took over the business in 1941 when Theodore died. The store was always known as Hutchie's. Samuel died in 1968, and the store closed for good that year. It was always a treat to go in and buy fresh chips. We would get a soda from the reach-in chest, on the left, when you entered the store, then get a 5-cent bag of chips. They would put the chips in a brown paper bag, and by the time we got home, the bag was soaked with grease.

Indigenous People

The sagamore around Salem, in 1629, had fewer than three hundred men. The number of subjects was large until the year 1617, when a fatal disease was so destructive that very few were left. The Tribes here were engaged in a great war with the Tarrantines from the eastward in the year 1615, which proved disastrous to the local tribe. Nanepashemet retreated from Saugus to a hill on the border of the Mystic River, where he later resided. Four years later, the Tarrantines killed him at his dwelling place. Gravesites offered many clues to the dates of burials. In Marblehead, objects were dated from before 1600, and many are pre-1500. Many arrowheads and stone implements found in the Naugus Head area of town date back thousands of years. All confirming that Marblehead was uninhabited at the time of settlement by the English in 1629.

Islands

Children's Island: By the late 1880s, the Children's Island Sanitarium was organized on Cat Island. The island, part of Salem, had many names and uses over the years. During the 1850s and 1860s, the area was known as Lowell Island, and a large, 100-room hotel was built and operated there. In 1878, Samuel Rindge purchased the property. Eventually, his son, Frederick H. Rindge, took ownership and donated the land to the Sisters of Saint Margaret for use as a sanitarium

Children patients on Children's Island

for children. It was believed that the sea air was great for healing ailments; therefore, the island made a great location for such a facility. They treated children with bone and joint diseases, malnutrition, rickets, and other noncontagious conditions. The sanitarium operated until 1946, on the island, and when it closed, the land went back to the Rindge family. Cat Island, or Children's Island, was leased by the Marblehead YMCA in 1955 for use as a summer day camp for children. The next year, the island was purchased by four Board Members of the YMCA. Over the years, plenty of work and maintenance has been done by the YMCA to keep up with storm damage on the exposed land. New buildings, a pool, a new pier, and other improvements have made the island a desirable location for campers, year after year. In 1996, the official name of the island was changed from "Cat Island" to "Children's Island".

Gerry Island: Priest's Island, Maverick's Island, Orne's Island, and Gerry Island are names of the island once owned by Thomas Gerry, whose son was Elbridge Gerry. A private home was on the Island until the 1970s, when the house burned down. You can walk to the island over the sandbar when the tide is out. Vehicles have also been driven out to the island.

Brown's Island: The Brown family owned this island for over 100 years. In 1918, it was sold to the Crowninshield family. Most locals still call it Brown's.

Joe Frogger

A Joe Frogger is a cookie, just a molasses cookie. Made famous by Lucretia Brown up on Gingerbread Hill, the cookie has become a favorite in Marblehead. Many places still sell them, but no one has the original recipe, despite what you may be told.

King's Rook

Howard Ferguson and Allen McMinn opened the King's Rook coffee house in 1959, at 12 State Street, with hours of noon to midnight. Before long, complaints from the neighbors forced a curfew to be imposed at 10 pm. Allen McMinn retired from the business around this time, and Howard Ferguson appealed to the Board of Selectmen to rescind the curfew. Ferguson put a sign on his coffeehouse door reading "Forced to close at 10 pm. May my neighbors rest in peace," which drew criticism from the Chairman of the Board of Selectmen and Police Chief Howard Magee. When the new license was issued in 1960, it had restrictions placed on it to appease the neighborhood.

Lafayette House

The Lafayette House is located at the intersection of Lee, Hooper, and Water Streets. It is said that the corner was cut off the house to make room for General Lafayette's carriage on his visit to Marblehead. Another rumor was that it was cut off to make room for the big wagons carrying rum! Great stories, but untrue. The house was built that way, as the foundation proves, most likely to let the rainwater rushing down Tucker Street pass by the house on the way to the harbor.

Lead Mill Hill

The Forest River Lead Company was established in 1840 on the Marblehead / Salem line on Lafayette Street, on the left as you entered Marblehead. In 1884, it became Chadwick's Lead Works and then Forest River Lead Works. The original building was destroyed by fire in 1897, and after rebuilding, it eventually became the National Lead Company. The Associated Grocers Cooperative of the North Shore Inc. purchased the property in 1946. Most of the small grocers in the area were part of the co-op, and with this new large warehouse space, it allowed the small stores to compete with the larger grocery chains. Storing food in an old building, most likely contaminated with lead, seemed like a good idea at the time, I guess! In February 1968, a fire leveled the building, and to this day, nothing has been built on the property. The hill on Lafayette Street, as you enter Marblehead from Salem, was often called Lead Mill Hill. Some of us still call it that.

Lee Mansion

In 1768, a large Georgian home was built for Jeremiah Lee, a wealthy merchant. Lee was probably the largest slave owner in Marblehead at a time when most of the residents were very poor. The Lee Mansion is now owned by the Marblehead Museum, and tours are offered in season.

Lighthouse

On October 10, 1835, a lighthouse was put into operation on Marblehead Neck. This white stone structure was only 23 feet high, but it was 53 feet above sea level. The ten lamps were fueled by whale oil when it was first operated. As buildings went up on Marblehead Neck, the old stone lighthouse was becoming barely visible from the sea. In 1895, it was decided to replace the old tower with a new, higher, metal-framed lighthouse that would stand 105 feet tall. The

Old stone lighthouse and keeper's house

new lighthouse was first lit in 1896. The property around the lighthouse was government-owned until Chandler Hovey purchased it in 1948 and donated the almost four acres to the Town of Marblehead.

Lumpy Lanes

Maple Lanes on Sewall Street in 1984

Marblehead had a few old bowling alleys over the years, but the most recent one was Maple Lanes at 14 Sewall Street. Nicknamed "Lumpy Lanes", this was a popular spot until it closed in 1984. Marblehead High School had gym classes that walked down there, and several leagues bowled there. Maple Lanes originally opened in 1942. The building is now the location of the National Grand Bank offices.

Lyceum

Lyceum Hall was built in 1844 at 71 Washington Street. This uniquely shaped building had a large hall with high ceilings on the second floor. There was a back entrance accessible from Mechanic Street. There were storefronts on the lower level, directly on Washington Street. The second floor was used for meetings and also served as a theater over the years. The building was in poor condition and was a safety concern when it was torn down in 1951.

Ma Toft's

William Toft opened a fruit store next to the railroad depot, at 93 Pleasant Street, in 1922. The store transformed into a smoke shop and candy store over the years. William's wife, Edna Mae Toft, also worked in the store, and after William died, she ran the store alone for fourteen years. Every kid in town knew the store and called it Ma Toft's. Edna worked in the store until she reached the age of seventy-nine, in 1963, when she closed the store. In 1963, the Caswell family opened "Caswell's Dairy Joy" in that location. They added sandwiches to the menu in 1965. In 1966, Caswell moved "Caswell's Restaurant" to 189 Pleasant Street into the space previously occupied by Sam Gale's Store.

Manataug Bottling Company

Manataug Bottling Company, also called Marblehead Bottling Company, was started in 1913 at Washington and Hawkes Streets by Frank H. Davis. The business was moved to 9 Cowell Street and was well known for its soda flavors, including Manataug Orangeade and Manataug Ginger Ale. Old bottles from the plant still turn up around town.

Marblehead Anniversaries

As you dig through Marblehead's history, you will hear about some of the large celebrations that were held in town. You may find an old Program Book from the 300th celebration from 1929. But wait, there is another Program Book for the 300th celebration from 1949! What gives? Of course, one is the anniversary of the town being settled by English colonist families (1629), and the other is for the incorporation of the Town and its being separated from Salem (1649). This means the Town is quickly approaching the 400th anniversary. I hope the Town celebrates like it did in the good old days. There was money left over from donations for the 350th in 1999. I'm sure that money has been carefully held for the next celebration, as it was designated.

Marblehead Deli

In July 1961, the Marblehead Delicatessen opened at 2 School Street. That was the place to go for a roast beef sandwich in the 1960s. They sliced the beef right in front of you. They also made a great hot pastrami sandwich.

Marblehead Mercantile

Marblehead Mercantile opened in 2022 and is a family-owned business specializing in unique Marblehead clothing and gift items. It is located at 132 Washington Street.

Marblehead Museum

Originally the Marblehead Historical Society, the group changed the name in 2003 to the Marblehead Museum & Historical Society to reflect its museum-quality collection and professional approach to exhibits, research, preservation, and education. The name was simplified in 2013 to Marblehead Museum. The Museum is located at 170 Washington Street.

Marblehead Pottery

Dr. Herbert Hall, around 1905, used pottery work in his sanitarium as therapy for the nerve disorders of his patients. This was the beginning of Marblehead Pottery. He recruited seventeen-year-old Arthur E. Baggs from New York to come to Marblehead to work with the patients. Baggs bought the pottery company from Dr. Hall in 1915 and opened a shop at 111 Front Street, in front of the old Sanitarium on Goodwin's Court. The pottery was also being made at the Devereux Mansion / Hall Sanitarium off Beach Street until 1923. Baggs closed the company in 1942, at which time the small shop at 111 Front Street was taken down. Marblehead Pottery became a collector's item and is still sought after by many.

Marblehead Submarine Base

Yes, Marblehead had a submarine base, but not the kind that housed undersea watercraft! This one made the best submarine sandwiches in town. It was located at 145 Pleasant Street and was run by the Roberts family from 1959 until 1972, when it changed management. As soon as you walked in the door, your eyes would water from the fresh-cut onions.

Martin, John S.

In 1886, John Sparhawk Martin started his wood, coal, lumber, and brick business at his wharf on Marblehead Harbor, on Cliff Street. John S. Martin Co. is still in the oil business at 65 Pleasant Street.

Martin's Coal Truck unloading bags of cement on Cliff street.

Mary Alley Hospital

When someone tells you that they were born in the Mary Alley Hospital, you have to ask them which one! The original or Old Mary Alley Hospital was on Franklin Street until 1953, when a new hospital was built on Widger Road. Keeping the same name

Mary Alley

confuses historians when there is a new building at a new location. I was born in the Mary Alley Hospital in 1953, oops, in the New Mary Alley Hospital. Some people born in 1953 were born in the old hospital! In 1965, they closed the maternity ward of the hospital, and in 1986, the hospital closed. The original hospital building was left to the Town of Marblehead in the will of Mary Alley.

Maverick

Moses Maverick had been granted permission to sell a "tun of wine" in Marblehead in 1638. He worked for Isaac Allerton and married Allerton's daughter, Remember. The Allertons came over on the Mayflower. In 1649, Maverick was elected to the first Board of Selectmen.

McClains

In 1913, Almon McClain had a new fish market building built on the land next to his house, at 36 State Street. McClain was a fisherman and an early boat owner in Marblehead. His daughter, Lottie McClain, married Chester Damon in 1914. Damon ran the fish market for years, and in 1955, the business was transferred to Damon's daughter, Elaine. In 1973, McClain's Fish Market closed its doors after more than 60 years in business at 36 State Street.

Almon McClain Fish Market at 36 State Street in 1914.

Mini Golf

"Marblehead Recreational Center Inc. presents Historic Marblehead in nine holes of miniature golf, opening Saturday, May 27, 1961, at 7 pm, weather permitting. Rear of Marblehead Laundry, 7 Lincoln Avenue." That was the mini-golf advertisement from the Marblehead Messenger newspaper on May 25, 1961.

Mino's

Mino's Roast Beef opened on Atlantic Avenue, at the corner of Hawkes Street, in 1971. The old Exxon gas station was there at the time, and the pumps were still out front. Archie was running the place and did a great job with the "late-night" crowd that would flock there when the bars closed. I believe they were originally open until 2 am on weekends. Mino's was always a prominent supporter of Marblehead sports teams. Mino's still exists in the same location, at 27 Atlantic Ave, in 2025.

Monuments

The Marblehead Seamen's Charitable Society erected a monument in 1848, on the top of Old Burial Hill, for deceased members. They only listed members' names that perished in the 1846 Gale, but the monument acts as a memorial for all of Marblehead's seamen who were lost at sea over the years.

On May 17, 1876, the town dedicated the Mugford Monument at the intersection of Pleasant and Essex Streets. It was on the one hundredth anniversary of the capture of the British transport Hope by Captain James Mugford, in the Continental schooner Franklin. Unfortunately, Captain Mugford was killed two days later, on May 19, 1776, in another battle outside of Boston. The monument was moved to Old Burial

Mugford monument dedication in 1876 at Pleasant and Essex Streets

Hill in 1912 by the Woodfin Express Company.

The Soldiers and Sailors monument, on Elm Street, was dedicated on July 4, 1876. This monument has the names of one hundred and thirty-eight soldiers and sailors, killed in wars. The inscription on one side reads "In Memory of Our Country's Defenders. 1776. 1812. 1861. Erected by the Citizens of Marblehead. Dedicated July 4, 1876." This monument was moved, in May 1913, to Pleasant Street, in what is now Memorial Park. The move was done by Frank W. Goodwin and his crew, and took five days to complete.

Movies

Hocus Pocus, Home Before Dark, Coma, Witches of Eastwick, Hubie Halloween, The Good Son, Midnight Mile, Pride of the Clan, Grown Ups, Grown Ups 2, and a few other movies contain scenes that were filmed in Marblehead. Oh, and don't forget "Lobster Fishing in Marblehead", a documentary film by Dan Dixey.

Muffin Shop

Luisa and Celeste Capasso opened a new store at 126 Washington Street in 1988 and named it The Muffin Shop. Today, in 2025, it is a popular meeting place for the locals and is still run by Luisa and Celeste.

Musters

Marblehead Musters are named after the process of mustering up a group of people to gather and fight fires. Originally, fires were fought with buckets of water, passed by hand down a line. Then, hand tubs were developed and pumped by hand to shoot a stream of water on the fire. They would occasionally test the equipment to keep it ready for fighting fires. Present-day Musters are competitions between hand tubs to see who can pump the longest stream. Marblehead still has the OKOs and the Gerry 5 hand tubs in Town.

Neighborhoods

Barnegat is the area around Little Harbor, and is where some of Marblehead's earliest English settlers lived. The first meeting house and burying ground were set up in this area.

The Shipyard, approximately from Chestnut Street to Hawkes Street, was where many ships were built.

May 4, 1709, in a court deposition, John Dixey mentioned "a place by ye name of Nogg's Head". He was referring to his neighborhood, next to Darby Fort, which was called the Darby Fort Side of Salem for several years. Dixey's neighborhood now had a name and, in time, the name transitioned into Naugus Head, the name still used today. There were also Chapel Pines, Ocean Park, Goodwinville, Peach Highlands, Devereux, Clifton, Reed's Hill, Downtown, Uptown, West Shore, Chinatown, The Neck, and others. Fewer and fewer people refer to areas by their neighborhood names today.

Nicknames

At one time, everyone in Marblehead had a nickname. I don't think people would have responded if you called them by their given names! Some of the hundreds I have on a list are: Turtle Adams, No Finger Atkins, Bottle Broughton, Half Past Six Bowden and Quarter to Seven Bowden, Blackboard Brown, Tippy Caswell, Cupcake Cameron, Tinker Carroll, Twofer Doliber, Rock Cod Dixey, Chummy Frost, Catgut Goodwin, Snotty Nose Hooper, Hot Pot Homan, Trousers Knight, Jack Ass Kiely, Cornball Martin, Coney Peach, Spark Plug Rodgers, Shoe Stick Roundey, Tom Teet Roads, Tow Horse Stephens, Cracker Stone, Shoe Fly Shattuck, Jumping Jack Sinclair, Pencil Woodfin, and so many more.

Old Town

Old Town is in Maine, not Marblehead. It is 238 miles from Abbot Hall. Although people know exactly where you are talking about, don't dare mention "old town" when speaking to a Header. If you don't believe me, ask Wayne.

Old Town House

In March 1727, the town voted to build a new meeting house at the site of the jail and cage in Market Square. The work was completed in 1728, and Marblehead now had a new meeting place. The Old Town House, as it is called today, still sits in Market Square at the intersection of Washington, Mugford, and State Streets. In 1836, to enlarge the space, the building was raised one level. A stone foundation and basement were added under the existing two-story structure. In 1856, the police department was set up, with a jail, in the basement of the Town House, under Chief John Dixey. In 1961, the Police Department moved out of the basement of the Old Town House. In 1976, a plaque from the US Department of Interior, National Park Service was mounted on the Old Town House, identifying the building as a National Register of Historic Landmarks. In 2012, money was approved to renovate and update the building, and to include an elevator. The following year, the work was completed, and the building was reopened with a working elevator for the first time.

Old Town House and trolley tracks

Outhouses

Outhouse, in center of photo next to the clothesline, at 14 Nicholson Hill

Before running water and plumbing were in houses, outhouses were often used. There were still some outhouses in use in Marblehead into the 1950s and probably a few even later. My grandparents' house on Nicholson Hill still had an outhouse when I was born in 1953.

Parades

At one time, Marblehead took pride in celebrating with large parades around town. Any large event that was planned included a parade. I have hundreds of old parade photos from various years. I think this is a tradition that should be brought back. A parade that lasts 10 minutes or less is not a real parade, by comparison.

Pharmacies

Some notable Pharmacies in Marblehead included: Tent's Pharmacy, Village Pharmacy, Shepard Pharmacy, Eaton The Druggist (2 locations), Beach Bluff Pharmacy, William M Lemmon Pharmacy, William C. Gregory Apothecary, Atkin's Pharmacy, Arthur N. Sumner Pharmacy, William Goodwin Pharmacy, Kenney Pharmacy, and others.

Points

See if you can find some of these Points in Marblehead! They include: Cloutman's Point, Fluent's Point, Doliber's Point, Peach's Point, Rockmere Point, and on the Neck: Stony Point, Foster's Point, Boden's Point, Jackson's Point, Flying Point, and Fishing Point.

Police Department

The town officially established a Police Department on April 11, 1853, when they appointed Adoniram Orne as the Chief of Police. Up until this time, the town had elected constables to enforce the laws. In the early years of the police force, the chiefs didn't remain for more than a year or two, in most cases. Some of the early chiefs had familiar names such as Orne, Pitman, Goodwin, Dixey, Tucker, Foss, Atkins, Gregory, Brown, Broughton, and others. The Police Station was in the basement of the Old Town House until a new building was built on Gerry Street in 1961 for police headquarters.

Politics

My cardiologist recommended I avoid stress, so I will keep this subject brief. The Town once had a group of people that worked together, helped each other, and built a close-knit community, making Marblehead a nice place to live with a small-town feel. This lasted into the late 1960s, early 1970s. The current political atmosphere now mirrors the national political scene. Two sides, fighting, without listening to each other, with no real debate. "I am right, you are wrong, so do as I say." The Town never let the State tell them how to run things in the past. Marblehead had character and guts. With the addition of social media, you now have keyboard warriors acting tough and slinging mud. Unfortunately, some social media groups allow anonymous posters, which is not helping matters. On Facebook, you can choose your side by joining either Anything Right 01945 or Everything Left 01945 (just my nicknames). If you don't want to listen to people preach online and want a stress-free environment, just join my Facebook group "Marblehead Historic Images," where the only conversations are about Marblehead history.

Pool Halls

There were several pool halls in business in Marblehead years ago. Notably, on Pleasant Street, there was one upstairs in the Rechabite Building and also one down in the Grader Block.

PHOTO: Fred Litchman center, Mike Grady on right outside the Pool Hall in the Rechabite Building on Pleasant Street

Poorhouses

A new almshouse, or poorhouse, was built on town land in 1851, after years of debate. The site chosen was behind the workhouse rocks, next to what is Vine Street today. The very first almshouse, in town, was built on Pond Street in 1726. Another poorhouse was built on Back Street, now Elm Street, in 1762. The town would house and feed the occupants and, when possible, find work for them.

Post Office

March 20, 1793, Marblehead opened the first Post Office in town. In the early days, mail would come into town twice a week. Residents would pick up their mail at a local post office location, and if their mail wasn't picked up, an advertisement would be placed in the newspaper notifying residents about their unclaimed mail. In the 1870s, it was located on Washington Street, across from the Lee Mansion. In 1879, the Post Office moved into the Odd Fellows Block on Pleasant Street. On October 1, 1906, a new Post Office and Custom House was built and opened at 59 Pleasant Street, on the corner of Watson Street. In 1975, construction started on a new Post Office building on Smith Street, and in 1976, the new facility was opened, and the Post Office moved from Pleasant Street.

Powder House

The town built a new brick powder house on the Ferry Road, now Green Street, in 1755. This structure was used to store the town's gunpowder safely away from the center of town and is still there.

Railroad

1839 was a turning point for Marblehead when the railroad rolled into town, connecting the town to the Salem branch. On October 19, 1871, the Eastern Railroad branch from Lynn was connected to the Marblehead track, bringing trains in from Swampscott and Lynn. In 1873, a new, larger train depot replaced the original building on Pleasant Street to accommodate the increased railroad traffic. The following year, a new depot was built on Devereux Street, and one at Clifton Station, adding additional stops in town. The 1877 fire burned down the Pleasant Street station, which was rebuilt and burned again in the 1888 fire. The next depot was made of brick and was the final building at the main depot on Pleasant Street. J. Archer

Dixey, Marblehead Selectman, placed a wreath on a train at the depot on Pleasant Street before it started up and left town in 1959. That was the very last commuter train to leave Marblehead, and it was the end of the railroad era in Marblehead

Realtors

Okay, I have a lot of friends who are realtors in Marblehead, but you may hear the following complaints. "Realtors are the ones that started using the term Old Town, just to sell houses", or "realtors are to blame for the overpriced real estate in Marblehead."! So, if you have a house to sell in Marblehead, say it's in "Old Town" and hire a realtor!

Redd's Pond

Redd's Pond was named for Wilmot "Mammy" Redd, the only Marblehead victim of the witchcraft hysteria. Most likely, her name was Reed, and she was married to a fisherman, Samuel Reed, who lived next to the pond. In May 1877, the town voted to make a reservoir of Redd's Pond, after years of the town rejecting this plan. Money was approved to run pipes into town and to place fire hydrants in appropriate locations. Elected to oversee the project were Adoniram C. Orne, Caleb Prentiss Jr., Hooper R. Goodwin, Isaac Atkins, and Thomas Appleton. The Marblehead Model Yacht Club was organized and met at Redd's Pond in 1892.

Restaurants

The Bide A Wee Tea Room was at 63 Front Street as early as 1921. By the 1930s, they were also serving breakfast, lunch, and dinner as "Bide-A-Wee". In 1953, they moved the restaurant from 63 Front Street to 146 Washington Street, at the corner of Darling Street. The restaurant was closed by 1973, when a dog grooming business moved into the building.
The Warwick Restaurant (Warwick Lunch) was opened at 114 Pleasant Street as early as 1938. In 1971, the business was changed to Blackbeard's Cove. Blackbeard's was shut down by the IRS for non-

payment of taxes in 1973. Super Sub moved to this location in 1974.
A MacDonald's Restaurant in Marblehead? Yes, but not the one with golden arches. In the 1940s and early 1950s, at 46 Smith Street, on the corner of Pleasant Street, was a MacDonald's Restaurant. In January 1946, Ken Duncan and his brother-in-law, Madison G. Putnam, were granted a beer and wine license by the Marblehead Board of Selectmen after a lengthy battle over a petition from the neighbors. Maddie's Sail Loft, restaurant and bar, opened at 15 State Street and became one of the most popular and iconic establishments in town. Maddie's is still in the same location today, in 2025.

Macdonald's Restaurant corner of Pleasant and Smith Streets. A fine colonial house with home-like atmosphere and a fireplace in every room. Our motto- Good Food. Open year round. For reservations telephone Marblehead 2620. Under the personal supervision of Mr. and Mrs. A. E. A. Macdonald.

Glover "Dill" Broughton opened his seafood restaurant at 141 Pleasant Street in 1946 and briefly called it Victoria's before changing the name to Dill's. Years earlier, in 1933, Broughton had applied for a license for a pool and billiard hall down the street at 116 Pleasant Street (now the Rip Tide), but the license was denied. The Three Cod Tavern, another great seafood restaurant, now occupies the space.
Brown's Bakery and Restaurant was located at 9 Atlantic Avenue in 1940. By 1980, they had moved into a building out back of 9 Atlantic Ave.
The Barnacle restaurant is at 141 Front Street, directly on Marblehead Harbor. The Barnacle has been in business in the same location since the late 1940s. Great restaurant and a great place to be during storms. The owner has his own lobster boat to provide fresh lobster to the restaurant.
In 1950, the Atlantic Restaurant opened at 40 Atlantic Avenue and was still operating there in 1974.

Nello's was a bar and restaurant in the 1950s and 1960s, at 259 Washington Street.

The Molly Waldo was at 12 School Street, and had its grand opening on May 20, 1954. Mildred and George Crowley ran the restaurant. In August 1972, the license was transferred, and it became the 76 Restaurant.

 Still, one of my favorite places to eat in Marblehead is the Driftwood Restaurant. It has the same feel as it did the first time we started eating there, over 50 years ago! Irving Duffy started this business as Duff's Driftwood on October 31, 1960, at 63 Front Street. This building was previously the Main Brace restaurant. Eventually, it was just known as The Driftwood. In the summer of 1969, the Driftwood opened an ice cream shop across the street from the restaurant on Front Street. It was called the Driftwood Dairy Bar. In 1981, Rocco and Marion Losano purchased the Driftwood Restaurant, previously run by Peggy Upchurch. Jan Frost started working there in 1970, and in 1982, Colleen Galvin joined the staff. When Rocco died in 2008, Colleen took over the restaurant. In October 2020, the Driftwood celebrated its sixtieth year in business in a quiet, pandemic way! Today, in 2025, when you walk in the door, you can still find Colleen, Tori, and occasionally Jan, though she officially retired in 2025.

 Romanos opened in 1965, at 28 Atlantic Ave., and was known for great Italian food. By 1984, they had moved to the Village Plaza.

The Landing Restaurant opened in 1972 at 82 Front Street. The restaurant is still open and has a public deck right on Marblehead Harbor.

Rosalie Harrington opened Rosalie's Restaurant in 1973 at 1 School Street. The restaurant later moved to 18 Sewall Street, into the old brick Metcalf Box Company and Daddy Scott Toy Company building. In 1983, Rosalie's was featured in a VISA credit card commercial on television, getting the restaurant some national exposure. The restaurant closed in 1995.

Antonio and Patricia Brogna opened Tony's Pizza at 1 School Street, in the brick Gregory Building, in 1981. I met Tony when he first opened, when I did some refrigeration work for him in the restaurant, and he was always a pleasure to work for. In February 2003, a large fire destroyed the old building and everything in it. Other businesses in the building were also wiped out, including photographer Rick Ashley. The businesses slowly rebuilt, and over two years later, in March 2005, a new building, the Brogna Building, was completed, and Tony was back in business in the same location. Unfortunately, Tony passed away on February 11, 2024. The family is still running the restaurant in 2025.

Sneakers Restaurant was at 9 Atlantic Avenue in the 1980s.

In the 1980s and 1990s, Jacob Marley's was a restaurant in Town. It started at 28 Atlantic Avenue and later moved to 9 Atlantic Avenue. Flynnie's on the Avenue was in business from 1995-2009, and Flynnie's at the Beach was open from 1990-2006. Everyone in town knows Jeff Flynn.

On May 1, 2007, the Percy family opened the Three Cod Tavern at 141 Pleasant Street. Dill's Restaurant was in this building for many years and was a well-known seafood restaurant. The Three Cod Tavern is a great restaurant specializing in New England seafood, continuing a tradition in this location. The separate bar is a good place to find some locals. It is still being run by the family, Chip, Marci, Gus, and Judd, today in 2025.

In 2019, entertainment entrepreneur Johnny Ray called his old friend Chef Edgar Alleyne to break the good news. "We finally have a spot, are you available?" The spot was 123 Pleasant St. in Marblehead, formerly the location of Wicks and Palmer's Restaurant. Designing began in earnest, and the Beacon brand was born. In June 2021, The Beacon opened, serving great food and weekly entertainment. In 2024, Johnny and Edgar formed a new partnership with local Marbleheader and Arizona businessman Curt Havens and Edgar's brothers Andrew and Ken Alleyne. The group now owns The Beacon Restaurant and Warwick Cinemas.

Some others were Jake Cassidy's, Sand Bar and Grille, Michael's House, Rinaldo's, Tar and Feathers, Peter's Sandwich Shop, Seafood Deli, and more.

Rip Tide

The Rip Tide is located at 116 Pleasant Street and has been there as early as 1952. Known as a "dive bar," most Headers in town had a drink served to them over that bar, at one time or another. I won't say how old I was when I had my first drink there. The building was sold and renovated in 2023 and reopened in 2024.

Sadie's

For fudge, we would walk down and see Sadie on Beacon Street, near Grace Oliver's Beach. We just went to a side door and placed our order, and got the fudge in a small paper bag.

Saltwater Bookstore

Saltwater Bookstore was established in May 2023 by long-time Marblehead resident, Laura Cooper. Saltwater's store is at 134 Washington Street, in a building that was built in 1790.

Samuel Roads

Samuel Roads Jr. published his "History and Traditions of Marblehead" book in 1880. This was a fantastic, detailed account of Marblehead's history, and has been the bible of historians since the day it was published. A revised edition of Roads History and Traditions of Marblehead was published in 1897. Roads also published many smaller booklets of Marblehead history.

Schoolhouses

Back Street School taught grades 1 to 3.

By 1767, the population in Marblehead was around five thousand people, and all the school buildings were reported to be in deplorable condition. The first national election took place in 1789, and George Washington took office as the first President of the United States.

That same year, the Marblehead Academy built a wooden building on Pleasant Street to be used as a school. The money was donated by Samuel Sewall, Robert Hooper, Samuel Hooper, William Raymond Lee, Elisha Story, Samuel Russell Trevett, John Humphreys, John Goodwin, Marston Watson, Richard Homan, Joseph Sewall, Samuel Bartol, John Dixey, Richard Pedrick, Ebenezer Graves, and Burrill Devereux. The town was dealing with financial hardships, and the residents included 459 widows and 869 orphans.

In the 1790s, Sea Captain John Marchant donated money to help the poor in Town, and the money was used to build a couple of schools. The Marchant School was built on Idler's Hill, the intersection of High and Back Streets (Back Street was renamed and is now Elm Street).

The town voted to establish a High School in Marblehead in 1837. Having only grammar schools in town, this High School would prepare older girls and boys for college. Boys and girls were taught in separate sections, much like the other schools. They rented space in the Masonic Lodge for their school rooms. They eventually moved high school students to the Marblehead Academy. Classroom space was limited at the Marblehead Academy, so in 1913, a new High School was built on Pleasant Street, at the top of the old workhouse rocks.

The Sewall School, on Spring Street, was built in 1856 and was remodeled in 1914. In 1934, there were two hundred and fifty students enrolled in grades one to five. The school was closed in 1936.

A two-and-a-half-story brick school was built at 140 Elm Street in 1880 and named the Story Grammar School, replacing the older wooden Story Grammar School building across the street. The school was named for Marblehead's Joseph Story, a Harvard graduate, Massachusetts State Representative, member of the U.S. Congress, and U.S. Supreme Court Justice. This school was the first brick schoolhouse in Marblehead and was the beginning of a commitment to better learning structures in town. The Story School closed as a school in 1978 and was converted into eight apartments, years later, in 1984.

In 1904, the two-story, brick Samuel Roads Jr. School was built on Rowland Street. When it was built, it was called the "new Barnard

Schoolhouse" but was renamed within a year to honor Marblehead's Samuel Roads Jr. Some people thought the town was overbuilding with this new school, but in 1905, it was at near full capacity. Class sizes ranged from 38 to 45 students per room. The Roads School at 26 Rowland Street closed as a school in 1981. In 1983, it was converted into town-owned apartments.

In 1906, the brick Elbridge Gerry School was built on Back Street (now Elm Street), replacing the old wooden Gerry Schoolhouse on High Street. The Gerry School was closed as a school in 2018, and the property was sold in 2020.

The new Farms School was built on the corner of Humphrey and Maple Streets in 1916. The neighbors petitioned for the name to be changed to the Clifton School, but the School Committee rejected the request. In 1918, the school was renamed the Glover School, being named after General John Glover.

The Tower School bought land in Marblehead in 1938 to move the school, which had been in Salem for 26 years.

L H Coffin School at 1 Turner Road was built in 1948. It was named after Lizzie H. Coffin. She was elected principal of the Story Grammar School in 1896, being the first female school principal in Marblehead. She was a 2nd grade teacher in Marblehead before that. The Coffin School closed in October 2021.

In February 1955, the new Junior High School was dedicated on Village Street. The building housed classrooms for seventh and eighth-grade students only. An addition was put on to the Junior High School in 1967. A new wing was added off the back of the school, and ninth-grade classes were taught here for the first time. The athletic fields were also added. This building is now the Village School.

Dr Samuel C Eveleth School was built in 1956 at 3 Brook Road. The school closed in 2015.

The Malcolm Bell School opened in September 1958, on Baldwin Road. The school welcomed two hundred students into the new kindergarten through sixth-grade classrooms. Construction of the new school at the site of the old Bell School started in 2020. The new mega-school at the old Bell School site, while still under construction in early 2021, was renamed the Lucrecia and Joseph Brown School.

In 1999, the town voted to appropriate the money to build a new High School, off Humphrey Street, near Tent's Corner. This major building project was completed, and the new school was opened in 2002.

The METCO Program was a school desegregation program started in 1966 and resulted from a report from the Advisory Committee on Racial Imbalance and Education. Seven suburbs in the greater Boston area took part in the program that first year. Marblehead signed up for the METCO Program in 1967 and was the first community on the North Shore and the furthest location from Boston to take part. Black students from seventh, eighth, and ninth grade from intercity schools rode on buses to the Marblehead Junior High School and the Star of the Sea School. The program was successful, and all the students taking part that first year, still living in the state, returned to Marblehead the following school year.

Seaside Park

The town voted, in 1895, to spend thirty-five hundred dollars to lay out a new park in town and chose land on Atlantic Avenue for the site of this new field. The land was leveled out, and in 1902, a baseball diamond was installed. This field was named Seaside Park and was enlarged in 1906 and again in 1913. The wooden backstop wall, behind home plate, was replaced with wooden bleachers in 1915 and 1916.

Seaside Park under construction

Sebastian Miniatures

In 1947, Prescott Baston and his son, Prescott "Woody" Jr., moved their store, with handcrafted Sebastian Figurines, or Sebastian Miniatures, from Arlington to 13 Bassett Street. They created molds of hundreds of people and subjects over the years in their shops in Marblehead and Arlington. They used to display their work in a picture window on Bassett Street.

Shoe Factories

There were too many shoe factories in Marblehead to list them all, but here are some notable ones.

Joseph Bassett ran a shoe factory in Marblehead, and as opportunity arose, after the railroad came into town, he wanted to expand his business. Bassett started buying up land, from School Street to Sewall Street, and up to Reed's Hill. The town and its residents were not happy about the new roads being laid out, and watched Bassett as he added house lots. Although the demand was not high for new houses, Bassett continued with his development. He built some modest houses on the lots and then offered these homes, for a fair price, to his employees. Bassett promised to keep them working as long as they lived in the houses, and he deducted the monthly payments from their paychecks. This was a great opportunity for the shoe workers to own a home, and it also put them in proximity to the shoe factory, near the depot on Pleasant Street. Bassett continued to purchase land, this time in the Commercial Street area of town. In 1847, he built a sawmill down by the water and was building his own wooden boxes, used to ship the shoes. Again, he started laying out roads and building homes for his workers. Even in tough times, Bassett kept his workers, as he had promised. This was a big turning point for Marblehead, with all the jobs and housing he created. It is estimated that he had hired over seven hundred people.

On February 5, 1867, a large fire burned down the shoe factory of Joseph Harris and Sons on Pleasant Street. A few other buildings were also destroyed, including the Baptist Church, next to the shoe factory. Harris had first opened his shoe business in 1841, in his house on Harris Court. After the fire, he moved and rebuilt a much larger building to accommodate his growing company, and chose a lot on Elm Street.

In 1897, John P. Goodwin was living at 30 Washington Street and, behind his home on Stacey Street, he had his carriage house. Across from the carriage house, off Stacey Court, Goodwin had a machine shop and a shoe factory. William E. Brown also had a shoe factory on Stacey Street.

With shoe businesses flourishing in 1890, a large Association Factory was built on Green Street. In 1891, a second Association Factory, building #2, was completed in the back of the Green Street property. In May 1937, the Association Factory #2 burned down. Towards the end, the front building housed a tape factory and Foster's Inc. Eventually, this building was removed, and houses now sit on the property. Humphrey and Paine Shoe Factory was at the intersection of Lincoln Avenue and Green Street, and Steven's Shoe Factory at 14 Atlantic Avenue. There were also F. W. & I. M. Monroe shoe factory, W. C. Lefavour shoe factory, Wormstead and Woodfin shoe factory, William Lefavour's shoe factory, and Woodbury Brothers' Shoe Factory.

Sorosis Farm

Sorosis Farm (not to be confused with Cirrhosis) was the largest farm in Marblehead. The Alexander E. Little Shoe Company of Lynn purchased close to four hundred acres of land in Marblehead for use as a farm. Originally called the Sorosis Military Farm, it was run by employees of A. E. Little and high school students preparing for the military. In 1917, the crews were building fences but were called in to answer to the Marblehead selectmen several times for building fences on town-owned property. The farm was named after the Sorosis shoes, produced in their Lynn shoe factory.

Sorosis Military Farm

The farm had many buildings scattered around its 400-acre property. There were sections fenced off for crops, animals, and poultry. The farm went bankrupt by the mid-1930s. When the Sorosis Farm owned land on Maple and Lafayette Streets, part of the gravel pit section was used for a dump site.

Spirit of '76 Painting

In 1880, John Devereux, a Marbleheader living in Cleveland, Ohio, purchased Archibald Willard's famous painting "Yankee Doodle", now commonly referred to as the "Spirit of 76", and donated it to the Town of Marblehead. Willard painted this scene in 1876 for a Philadelphia Exhibit, during their centennial celebration, and it was the original painting. Willard painted other copies of the scene later. The painting depicts two drummers and a fife player marching through a battlefield. The significance of the musicians in these wars is rarely understood. The drums and fife could be heard for a distance, and were used to keep the soldiers organized, and would signal for certain maneuvers to be made. The model used for the young drummer in the painting was Devereux's son. The painting was hung in the reading room, in Abbot Hall, where it still hangs on display today.

Storms

John Avery was a preacher in England, and he came to the colonies in 1634. Marblehead invited him to organize a church in town, but he declined and settled in Newbury. The following year, he took the offer in Marblehead and, along with his wife and children, loaded the family's belongings onto a boat in August 1635. Joining Avery on the sail down from Newbury to Marblehead was his cousin Anthony Thacher and his family. A violent storm was encountered during the trip, and the ship was wrecked on some rocks off Cape Ann. Thacher and his wife survived by swimming to a nearby island beach, but they were the only survivors. The island is now named Thacher Island.
Later named "The Portland Gale," a storm hit the New England coast on November 26 and 27, 1898, and caused considerable loss of life and property damage. The steamship "SS Portland" was on a return trip to Maine from Boston when she got caught in the storm. The ship went down, and all 192 passengers and crew were lost. Another 200 lives were lost along the coast because of the storm, mostly in boating accidents.
On Sunday, March 1, 1914, a storm with heavy rains soaked Marblehead. An inadequate drainage system in the Shipyard section could

not handle the water flow, and a major section of Commercial, Central, and Chestnut Streets was flooded. People were stranded in their houses, basements were full of water, and some areas had up to five feet of water in the street. Rowboats were used to get people out of their homes and onto dry ground. New drains were installed in May and June to prevent any future flooding.

The New England Hurricane of 1938 was a Category 3 storm that caught everyone off guard in late September. It was one of the most powerful storms to hit Marblehead.

Another powerful storm, Hurricane Carol, hit Marblehead on August 31, 1954, and caused considerable damage in town.

Boat beached on Fort Beach after hurricane, September 21, 1938

The Blizzard of '78 hit New England on February 6 and 7, 1978, dumping over two feet of snow in most areas. The town was paralyzed, along with surrounding communities, and people could not use their cars after being ordered to stay off the streets.

There was the No Name Storm and Hurricane Bob.

A fast-moving microburst moved through Marblehead on July 31, 2019, causing major damage. The "tree" at Fort Sewall was badly damaged. The most photographed tree in town did not survive and was eventually taken down.

Super Sub

In September 1971, the Board of Selectmen issued a Common Victualer License to Alfred Mattei for a sandwich shop, called Super Sub, at 96 Washington Street. The shop moved to 114 Pleasant Street, and Ben Rhodes held a grand opening there in February 1974. Super Sub was a favorite with the locals and a great place for breakfast for some town workers. Ben and Howie knew everyone and would start preparing your order before you placed it. Many of the "regulars" had a coffee mug with their name on it hanging on a shelf near the counter.

Ben closed the shop in 2013, and Hooked Seafood and Grille went into the space.

Swearing

Swearing was a standard component of the Marblehead dialect over the years. Not overused, but spoken often enough to make a point. In 1893, there was a Marblehead Anti-Swearing League. Read all about it in the Marblehead Messenger newspapers from 1893 and 1894! Today, I don't condone profanity. So don't be a f****** a******!

Ten Footers

Ten Footer at the base of Fountaon Park

Marblehead was heavily involved in the popular shoe business, and there were many small, backyard sheds used for making shoes. Fishermen would use the sheds when they weren't working out at sea. These small buildings were called ten-footers and usually had some kind of wood-burning stove to keep them warm in the winter.

Tent's Corner

Tent's Corner at Pleasant, Humphrey, and Lafayette Streets circa 1940s.

James Tent opened a pharmacy at 1 Humphrey Street, at the intersection of Humphrey and Lafayette Streets. It was named "Tent's Pharmacy," and because of the name, the intersection became known as Tent's Corner. It was there as early as 1944. In 1975, the business was changed to Marblehead Pharmacy. Most Headers still call that intersection "Tent's Corner". Marblehead Bank is now located there.

Think Rink

In February 1968, a group was formed with the goal of building an ice-skating rink for Marblehead, Swampscott, and Salem. A piece of land near Vinnin Square was the prime location to make this happen, and Think Rink had begun their planning. Bumper stickers were seen on many cars, and it was the topic of conversation among the hockey players and ice skaters in the three communities. Neighborhood opposition was the biggest barrier, as usual. In December 1975, as the bumper stickers faded, so did the dream of many. The plan faded away, but came alive again in 1998 when "Skate 98" was formed to make another attempt at building a rink in town. Today, in 2025, there are still people who would love to make this happen.

Timmie's

Timmie's Hot Dog Stand at Devereux Beach was a favorite place to grab a quick bite or cold drink while at the beach. The stand first opened in the 1930s and was run by Tim Cahill for 41 years. Cahill was allowed the concession stand at the beach in exchange for policing the area. Timothy Cahill was born in Marblehead on October 20, 1881, and lived to the age of 96.

Timmie's place at Devereux Beach on Tuesday, August 26, 1958. Razed in 1967.

Traffic

When I was young, growing up in Marblehead, traffic and parking were not issues. My grandparents, along with other families in Town, never even owned a car. We learned to ride our bikes on Bessom Street, long before Village Plaza was built. As the town started getting richer, families started buying two cars. Then, not wanting to upset the spoiled children, a third car, or more, was added to the family. In the 1960s, after the trains stopped running, anyone leaving town had to now drive to their destination. With the narrow streets and cramped housing layouts, the town was never able to easily handle the extra traffic. Even when the population wasn't growing, the number of cars on the road surged in numbers. This problem only gets worse as additional housing units are built.

USS Constitution (Old Ironsides)

The USS Constitution had been on a mission to the West Indies when several issues with the ship forced it to return to Boston. To avoid the British ships outside of Boston, they landed north at Cape Ann on April 2, 1814. The next morning, they pulled anchor and hugged the coast while heading down towards Boston. They quickly spotted two British frigates, HMS Tenedos and HMS Junon, approaching. The wind direction made it impossible to outrun the heavily armed frigates, so they decided to attempt to seek shelter in the next harbor, at Marblehead.

USS Constitution in Marblehead Harbor in 1931

Captain Charles Steward, in command, was not familiar with that section of the coast or the entrance to the harbor. Knowing his crew was comprised of many Marbleheaders, he looked for someone to take over the ship. The name of Samuel Harris Green was conveyed to him, and he recruited Green to bring the USS Constitution into Marblehead Harbor. Green was born in Marblehead, was the son of a mariner, and began sailing at an early age. He had captained many large merchant vessels in and out of Marblehead over the years, but never under pursuit of the British Navy. Thirty-one-year-old Green was a quartermaster on this ship and was recovering from a severe leg injury. He still took the helm and piloted the Constitution safely into the harbor, with the coast lined with onlookers and armed recruits ready to engage the British ships. The two frigates backed off and eventually left, then the Constitution was moved into the safer harbor in Salem. The USS Constitution again visited Marblehead Harbor in 1931 during a fundraising tour. She returned to Marblehead in July 1997, when the 1500-ton, wooden battleship made the trip on the 200th anniversary of its first launching.

Village Plaza

On April 17, 1969, a front-page story in the Marblehead Reporter announced plans were in the works for the building of a two-story brick shopping mall at the corner of Pleasant and Bessom Streets.

1978

1978

A realty trust led by Ed Shinn and State Rep. Hilary Rockett would develop the new Village Plaza. Shinn owned the Village Rug, also on Bessom Street, and said this new shopping center would hold 16 stores and have parking for one hundred cars. Some people believed the town already had more businesses than it could support, but the project was built as planned. The old Nelson's Funeral Home, which was then the Village Decorator on the corner of Pleasant and Bessom Streets, had to be moved down Bessom Street. Also, a couple of houses on Pleasant Street had to be taken down to make room for the new building and parking lot. The plaza opened in January 1970 with the following stores on the first floor: Village Pharmacy, Sam's Cleaners, Cambridge Coffee Tea & Spice House, White Hen Pantry, and Brigham's Ice Cream.

Walton

Around 1638, a meeting house was built on the top of Old Burial Hill, and they also began using that land as a burial ground. William

Walton moved to Marblehead and would become Marblehead's first minister, preaching in this new meeting house. Walton was unordained, but served as a trusted preacher in Marblehead for thirty years. Walton's house was believed to have been near the base of Old Burial Hill, near Little Harbor. There was a spring flowing behind his house, which was referred to as Walton's Spring. In October 1668, William Walton died after serving as Marblehead's preacher for thirty years. Samuel Cheever was hired to replace Walton, and in 1684, Cheever was ordained. William Walton is my 9th great-grandfather.

Wars

You couldn't find a more patriotic town than Marblehead, over the years, for serving their country. They were often the first to respond to a call to duty. Many men and women from Marblehead have served in every war the USA has participated in. We all know that if it wasn't for Marbleheaders bailing out George Washington in 1776, we would still be flying the British flag in this country!
During the War of 1812, Marbleheaders, that lost their lives in Dartmoor Prison, were John Adams Jr. the son of John and Sarah, Thomas Jarvis the son of John and Elisabeth, John Kelly, Joseph Lackey the son of Andrew, Richard Lee the son of Richard, Joseph Widger the youngest son of William and Elisabeth and thirty-two-year-old Captain Thomas Courtis who left behind his wife Hannah Vickery Courtis and two children.
When the Civil War ended, in 1865, the following Marblehead men had died: William Hunt, Francis Freeto, Francis Joseph, Nathaniel R. Blaney, George B. Bartlett, Peter Crowley, William P. Lecraw, Thomas Cox, William S. King, Charles E. Roache, Edwin S. Rundlett, Andrew Colford, Eben Collyer, Moses P. Graves, Richard Prior, John Sandwich, Nicholas Twisden, Samuel H. Doliber, Samuel J. Goodwin, William H. Johnson, Robert McCully, William Tindley, Andrew Madison, Archelaus S. Ross, Benjamin F. Roundey, Wilson Russell 3rd, John H. Savory, Archibald Sinclair, David Steele, Benjamin B. Swasey, Philip A. Sweet Jr., William B. Sweet, Burrill Witham, Charles E. Lyon, Michael Graves, John Ragan Jr., William Bessom,

Nicholas Bessom, William F. Doliber, William Brown, George W. Ramsdell, Bartholomew Cahill, Alexander S. Standley Jr., Thomas P. Atkins, Oliver Chinn, Peter Welsh, Samuel Goodwin, Daniel B. Haskell, William McCormick, Robert C. Cahill, John Hines, William Donovan, Thomas Brown, William E. Philips, James Keith, Nicholas Bartlett Jr., John Grant, Edward Smethurst, Michael Hennessy, John Butman, William Peachy, John Goss, John Ingalls, Daniel S. Millett, William Bartol, John Sullivan, John Woodfin, Nathaniel Gilley, George Jones, Richard Chapman, Francis Rathburne, Charles Flint, Michael Casey, Peter Collins, Michael McCoy, Jacob Alley, Joseph Collyer, Gardner Goodwin, Richard Gardner, Robert Grieve, Thomas Oliver, Thomas Kelley, John Donovan, John Flynn, Ambrose Goss, Thomas Russell, John Goodwin Jr., Gamaliel Morse, William Terhune, John Shaw, Thomas Peach Jr., Richard Caswell, John Crommett, Theodore Wormstead, Francis Ireson, Richard Martin, William Bartlett, William O'Neill, Henry Rennard, William Brown, Richard Laskey, Samuel Martin, Daniel Ragan, Christian Dorien, John Green, John Brown, William Brown, William Garney, William Wooldredge, Thomas Stevens, William Adams, Jonathan Blaney, Benjamin Cloutman, and John Curtis.

In World War I, Marblehead lost six men, either from injury or illness. They were Charles Herbert Evans, John Alexis Roundy, William Francis Farry, Irving Eugene Brown, John McGee, and Christian S. Christensen. The war ended on November 11, 1918, when Germany formally surrendered.

The World War II Marbleheaders that died from the war were: Richard W. Ahlman Jr., James S. Bailey Jr., Clifford G. Barry, Sidney A. Benson, James E. Brophy, Charles L. Carlson, John W. Clark Jr., Frederick T. Clive, John F. Conners, Laurence M. Courtis, Lawrence W. Crozier, John J. Cudihy, Benjamin Cunningham, Charles A. Dana, Roger W. Dennis, Willard W. Fader, Azor O. Goodwin, Pembroke T. Hamilton, Norman E. Henderson, Wallace F. Hooper, Donald E. Howie, Paul L. Jacobson, Antoine W. Lausier, William J. Loveday, Reverend Thomas M. Mark, Arthur J. McNulty. William K. Melzard, Ralph T. Messervey, Richard A. Messinger, Paul W. Monahan, David A. Nye, Herbert S. Polley, John H. Ramsey, George H.

Shube, Arthur D. Somes Jr., Arthur L. Stout, Benjamin G. Tassinari, Alfred R. Tenny Jr., Richard H. Treat, Herbert F. Tuxbury Jr., Hale Very, and Edwin F. Walsh. The war officially ended in September 1945.

Another war broke out in 1950, and this Korean War lasted three years. The Marblehead men losing their lives because of this conflict were Joseph E. Caruso, Donald L. Davis, Raymond Foss, and Robert R. Bisbee.

November 1, 1955, was the beginning of the Vietnam War, a war that lasted twenty years. This war took Marbleheaders' lives and had serious health consequences for many more. Lost due to the Vietnam War were: John C. Archbold, Warren W. Boles, Edgar S. Doliber, Tristan W. Hayes, Gerald E. Isaacson, Henry E. MacCann, Duncan B. Sleigh, and Warren P. Smith Jr.

Army Staff Sergeant Christopher Neal Piper, of Marblehead, died June 16, 2005, from wounds sustained from an improvised explosive device detonated near his convoy in Orgun-E, Afghanistan, during Operation Enduring Freedom.

Warwick Theater

Warwick Theater on Pleasant Street

In August 1916, land on Pleasant Street at the old brick pond reservoir was sold to the Warwick Theater. A movie theater was built and tickets went on sale in April 1917. The theater was remodeled in 1949. The theater was family-owned and run by the McNulty family. In 1999, Tom McNulty closed the Warwick Theater on Pleasant Street after over eighty years of the family operating the business. The building was converted into a gymnastics center for the YMCA, and then, in 2011, the building was torn down. The Warwick Cinema reopened in the same location, at 123 Pleasant Street. In 2024, Johnny Ray and Edgar Alleyne formed a new partnership with local Marbleheader and Arizona businessman Curt Havens and Edgar's brothers Andrew and Ken Alleyne. The group now owns The Warwick Cinemas.

Wharfs

In 1933, the Graves Yacht Yard purchased the Stearns & McKay Yacht Yard property at 89 Front Street on Marblehead Harbor, next to Dixey's Wharf. Stearns had a boatyard and railway as early as 1895 in that location.

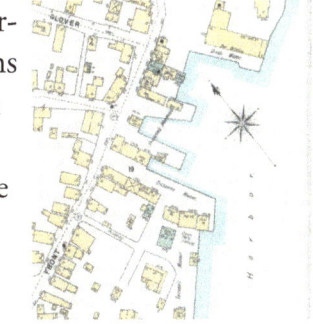

Tucker's Wharf and State Street Wharf are the most familiar wharf names. Tucker's Wharf is the area around Marblehead Transportation Company or the Harbormaster's Office. State Street Wharf is on Front Street across from the end of State Street. The project of filling in part of the State Street Wharf was underway in 1976. The project was done in phases and filled in two sections of the water, where it came up to Front Street. The work expanded the land and parking lot on Front Street and added some much-needed parking spaces.

In 1886, John S. Martin started his wood, coal, lumber, and brick business at his wharf on Marblehead Harbor, on Cliff Street.

Whip

Whip is a Marblehead term that has various meanings. It was mostly used as a greeting between Headers. If you were at sea and someone from a passing ship yelled "whip", you knew where they were from. An old Marblehead newspaper article may explain how the term came about. "A version of the origination of the word 'Whip' is that it alludes to a certain salve that Peter Cortee used when shoeing horses in his blacksmith shop on what is now Essex Street. This salve, first called "whipping salve," later gained some renown for its medicinal qualities." Could whipping salve have been the drug of choice for some locals?

Winslow's

Winslow's Chip store on Lincoln Ave and Green Street

Winslow Chip Company was founded by Henry C. Winslow in 1932. In 1937, they moved into a new factory on Green Street, at the intersection of 2 Lincoln Avenue. They remained in business through the 1960s and were one of the largest chip producers in New England. Cran Barry moved into the building in 1967.

Yacht Clubs

The Marblehead Boat Club, located on Cliff Street, was founded in 1878. They incorporated and changed the name to Marblehead Yacht Club in 1935.

The Bay View Boat Club was organized on July 25, 1881, and incorporated on January 31, 1887. They were at the end of Goodwin's Court for years, and also used a building on Front Street, near the State Street wharf.

The Eastern Yacht Club started with twelve men in March 1870. In 1881, the EYC clubhouse building was completed on Marblehead Neck.

Corinthian Yacht Club on Marblehead Neck

The Corinthian Yacht Club was organized on Marblehead Neck on July 7, 1885, to establish racing among some of the smaller sailing crafts in Marblehead. The certificate of incorporation was filed on January 17, 1888.

The Pleon Yacht Club was started on Marblehead Neck by a group of boys in 1887. It was one of the earliest "junior yacht clubs" organized.

The Burgess Boat Club was formed in 1894 and was on Goodwin's Court. The members merged with the Boston Yacht Club in 1902, when they opened their Marblehead clubhouse.

The Boston Yacht Club was organized in 1866 in Boston. The Marblehead BYC opened in a building next to the State Street Wharf at 73 Front Street in 1902. They purchased the property at 1 Front Street in 1956 and moved to that location, where they remain in 2025.

The Dolphin Yacht Club was formed in 1950 and incorporated in 1951. Being denied services by some existing clubs on Marblehead Harbor, a group of Jewish men thought it was best to start their own club to "promote and foster the nautical spirit among its members regardless of color, race, or creed." Originally in a space at the Rockmere Hotel property, the club is now on Allerton Place.

The Rockmere Hotel, by 1958, housed the Quarterdeck Yacht Club.

The Marblehead Model Yacht Club was organized and met at Redd's Pond in 1892. The club encouraged the building and sailing of model sailboats, a tradition still witnessed on Redd's Pond today.

YMCA

The local YMCA was established in 1859 and occupied a space in the Marblehead Academy building on Pleasant Street. After a few other locations, in 1888, the YMCA purchased the King Hooper Mansion. They moved their facility to this property at 8 Hooper Street. In 1910, for $2400, they purchased land on Pleasant Street across from the railroad depot. A new YMCA building was built there. In December 2008, the current building was completed on Leggs Hill Road, and the YMCA moved to this current location.

The Farm Store was Penni's Market (before 1945 fire)

American House on the corner of Washington Street and Atlantic Ave in 1898. This hotel had many owners and at one time was the only hotel in town. It was later called the Hotel Gerry.

Coralie Mason, Alice Nicholson and Lynda Chapman riding bicycles in 1898

Burgess Plant at Gas House Beach. Gazebo at Old Burial Hill seen in background on left.

Marblehead Harbor circa 1906

Spite House, Orne Street with water pump on right.

Adams House Restaurant in 1898. Mrs John T Adams, Jennie Stacey, Lena Hare and John T Adams

Adams House and Barnacle restaurants on Front Street

Ed Haley's Public Market on Washington Street. Women lined up to purchase rationed products during the War.

Salkins and Laskey in the Mugford Building on Washington Street. First traffic light pictured.

National Grand Bank, 2 Hooper Street, in Bank Square

Fred Litchman Photographer, Marblehead Laundry, J Wormstead Paint on State Street

White and Company on Washington Street in Bank Square

Thompson's on Washintgton Street in 1958

Brown's Bakery and Restaurant at 9 Atlantic Ave circa 1970

Bide-A-Wee Restaurant on corner of Washington and Darling Streets in April 1967

William F Stanley Clam Shop at 8 Orne Street, 1942

View towards Marblehead Neck from Old Burial Hill

2 Banks in Lee Mansion on Washington Street

Osborne Grocery Store on Pleasant and School Streets

Martin's Dairy truck

Horse drawn ice truck

West Shore Drive in its early days

Green Street near Kenneth Road from corner of Naugus

Hinkley Building on the corner of Washington and Pleasant Streets. Removed in 1870

Fort Beach with Fort Sewall in the background in 1875.

Walter Williams Dentist office, later Nelson's Funeral Home on corner of Pleasant Street and Bessom Street. Later moved up Bessom Street as part of Village Plaza project

Herbie Dale's Liquor Store, corner of State and Front Streets in October 1958

State Street Wharf in March 1957

Harold and Elsie Hammond at Gordon's Store at 111 Washington Street in 1950

Jack Sinclair, street sweeper, on May 28, 1914 on State Street.

C Eustis in 1901 in Bank Square

Fred Vining and friends pitching pennies at the State Street landing. Chester's Liquor Store, run by Chester Kuszmar, at the corner of Front and State Streets in 1956.

Howards News next to Super Sub on corner of Pleasant and School Streets

Redd's Pond early model sailboats

Hector's Pup, corner of Washington and State Streets

Goodwin's Store at 4 Washington Street

J Lawrence Rodgers, Alice Rodgers Hardwick, Theodore Bud Hardwick in front of Rodgers Ice Cream at 7 School Street in the Gregory Building.

Wagon of the William F. Cloon Hardware store. The store was located at 86 Washington Street, on the corner of State Street. The wagon is in front of the Gun House on Back Street (now named Elm St). In the wagon, with the derby hat, is Horace Cloon, son of William F Cloon and Deborah Proctor, the driver is William Martin, with an unidentified woman and child in the middle. Horace was born in 1861 and the photo is circa 1880s.

Harbor side of Marblehead Neck

Adams House and Fort Sewall circa 1897

Damon Tucker's store on Atlantic Ave. in 1956

Old Catholic Church at Prospect and Rowland Streets

St Michael's Church

The Delta ferry boat approaching the dock at Marblehead Transportation Company in 1938.

View of School Street and new Fire Station from Pleasant Street. Taken between 1877 and 1888

Pumper and fire crew on Franklin Street on July 4, 1884

Moses Allen Pickett handtub on Franklin Street

Franklin Street Fire House in 1908. The driver of the wagon is Butch Hammond, L-R Lou Pedrick, Christy Burridge, Bill Chamberlain, Rob Hammond, Henry Martin, Jaby Stacey, Bill "Kaiser" Atkins, Will Sweet, Ben Sweet and Charlie Stacey. The horses name is Mr Boston.

Gerry 5 hand tub on Washington Street. Jacker Hammond standing on machine. Man on left is Dibbie Day Hammond and next to him is Fred Brown. Third from right, with both hands in pockets, is Cracker Stone.

Horse Drawn Fire Apparatus in front of Central Fire Station on School Street

Engine 2 at Central Fire Station on School Street in June 1942

Gerry 5 pumper testing at Redd's Pond. 1991

Fire at the old Lead Mill on Lafayette Street in 1968.

Moving house up State Street in front of Frost's Bakery

View towards Marblehead Light Plant from Marblehead Neck. Old Catholic Church in center (on Prospect and Rowland Streets)

Gilbert and Cole on Bessom Street next to railroad tracks

Gilbert and Cole delivery wagon

Spanish American War soldiers training at Naugus Head in 1898.

Fort Miller on Naugus Head in 1898

Fort Miller on Naugus Head in 1898

Soldiers at Fort Miller on Naugus Head in 1898

Spanish American War Soldiers at Fort Sewall in 1898. This was the last time it was manned as a fort.

Towns people gathered around the Town House steps with men ready to go off to War in 1917. Ezekiel Peach is third row back on the left.

Maddie's Sail Loft and Marine Exchange East on State Street in 1992

The Sea Gull corner of Washington and Darling Streets in 1992

Marblehead Harbor circa 1900

Marblehead Harbor circa 1900

Forest River Lead Works, Lafayette Street

Jack and the Spades, 1960s. Jack Brooks, Mike Dixey, Doug Hill, and Ed Waliakis

In 1973, McClains Fish Market closed it's doors after more than 60 years in business at 36 State Street. Pictured left to right are: the owner Elaine Damon, Everett Goodwin and Norman Vincent. Elaine took over the business from her father, Chester Damon

Presidential Yacht, USS Mayflower in M'head Harbor, 1923.

Conly & Hooper store on Front Street

Sorosis Farm buildings at current High School property

Village Street looking east.

High Street

Looking up Elm Street from near the intersection of Sewall Street.

Policemen walking in front of Litchman's on Washington Street

The Devereux Mansion, on Beach Street, was once used as a hotel. Later it was used as a sanitarium and was where they first made Marblehead Pottery as a therapy for the patients.

Gerry Island

Causeway and Marblehead Neck with Nanepashemet Hotel to the left

Marblehead Electric Trolley

Devereux train depot on Devereux Street

Clifton train station

Marblehead's first Railroad Station on Pleasant Street, built 1839.

Pleasant Street train depot before 1877 fire

Pleasant Street train depot circa 1900

Clarence "Doanie" Doane in July 1960 toasting the demise of the railroad depot and end of train service

Eastern Yacht Club in 1938

William Lemmon drugstore on Washington Street, across from the Old Town House in 1938.

The Sou'wester and an Antique Shop on Front Street, looking from end of State Street towards Glover Street in 1938.

Peach's shanty at Graves Boat Yard in 1938

View towards Marblehead Neck across Front Street and Fort Sewall from Fountain Park in 1938.

View from Castle Rock on Marblehead Neck in 1938.

Marchant Schoolhouse on High and Elm Streets

Sewall School on the corner of Spring and Elm Streets. Built in 1856.

Gerry Island from Fort Sewall

"Save the Gerry School" rally in 1991

Francis Humphreys Shoe Factory on Pleasant Street

Clydesdale Truck on Washington Street in front of the Marblehead Savings Bank. Lillibridges Lunch sign is on the left, behind the truck.

Association Factories off Green Street

Association Factory shoe workers

This baseball game was played on August 1, 1914 at Seaside Park. Marblehead lost to Salem by a score of 8-2. Marblehead players were: N. Kenney (3b), Chapman (lf), Haller (cf), Skilton (p), Weed (1b), J. Kenney (ss), Linberg (rf), Sullivan (2b), and Osborne (c). The old catholic church at the intersection of Prospect and Rowland Streets can be clearly seen in the background. Atlantic Avenue is lined with horse drawn carriages and early motor vehicles. The bare spot on Atlantic Avenue to the right center is where the new catholic church was built in 1928.

Football game at Seaside Park circa 1920s

Water lines being installed on Green Street, circa 1880s. Facing towards Pond Street, the house on the right is 20 Green Street.

Water lines being installed on Back Street, circa 1880s

Water stand pipe being assembled and installed up behind Vine Street circa 1891. This was removed in the 1960s.

Franklin Street (circa 1915 -1920) with trolley tracks running down to the end of Selman Street. All the way down on the right is an electric trolley on the track.

Boats on Rockmere Beach after Hurricane Carol, 1954

Front Street looking towards the Adam's House after storm in 1898

Horribles Parade on Washington Street in the 1870s. The first building on the left was the Post Office and Abbot Hall would be built soon, on the left at the top of the hill.

Group in front of National Grand Bank on Hooper Street

Taken from Lee Street, looking towards Washington Square circa 1880s. Behind the tree, at 199 Washington Street, you can see part of the sign on John H Haskell's grocery store. On the right of this photo is 61 Lee Street, which was owned by John Bartlett.

Flood on Central and Chestnut Streets. March 1, 1914

Sorosis Farm dump site at Maple and Lafayette Streets

Hathaway Purington Truck, locally built, parked in front of the National Grand Bank at Bank Square in 1923. Lillibridge's Restaurant and a Laundry seen in background on the corner of Darling Street.

BUSINESS NOTICES.

HUMPHREYS & TWISDEN,
DEALER IN
WOOD, COAL, LIME AND CEMENT,
Marblehead.

WILLIAM KERR,
Wholesale and Retail Dealer in

WATCHES AND JEWELRY,
Silver Ware,

French Clocks, Musical Boxes, &c.

39 Hanover Street, Boston.

☞ Good Warranted as represented.

WILLIAM C. GREGORY,
PHARMACIST,
Corner School and Essex Streets,
Marblehead.

☞ Prescriptions carefully Compounded.

FOWLER & KENDALL,
Auctioneers, Commission Merchants
Real Estate Brokers and Insurance Agents,
Office, 139 Washington St.
Salesroom, 34 Front St.   Salem.

B. D. DIXIE,
DEALER IN
Lykens Valley, Ben. Franklin, Red Ash;
Excelsior, Enterprise and Big
Mountain White Ash

COALS,
Also Hard and Soft Woods,
57 Front Street.   Marblehead.

WILLIAM SPARHAWK,
DEALER IN
FAMILY GROCERIES
Flour, Grain, Provisions,
CROCKERY AND GLASSWARE,
4 Waldron Street, Marblehead.

1881

Coralie Mason, Alice Nicholson and Lynda Chapman on rock in Clifton in 1898.

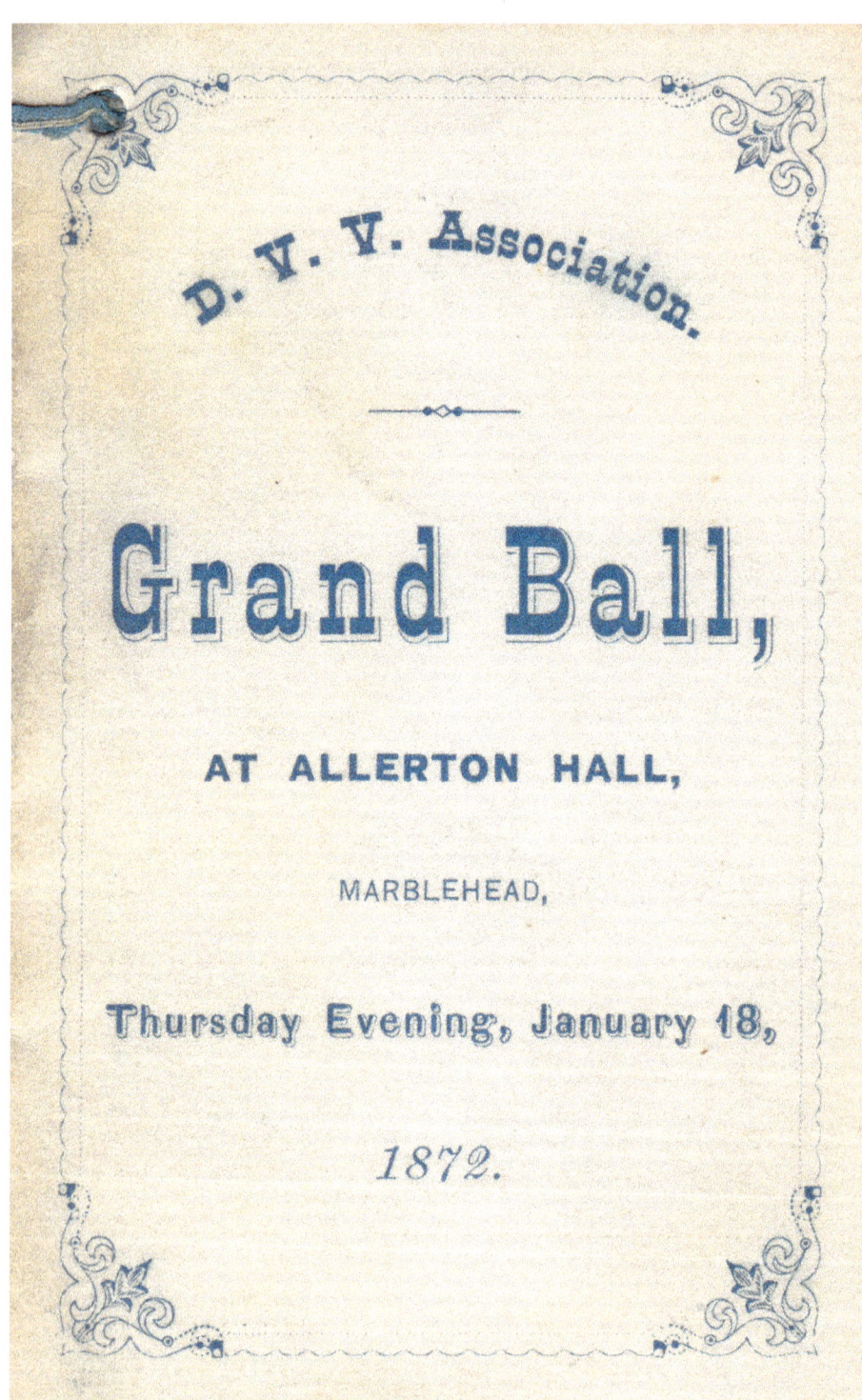

Harbor View Dari Whip on February 1, 1957. Run by Doris Perry Slattery at 63 Front Street (Driftwood is there now)

Parade on Washington Street in 1956.

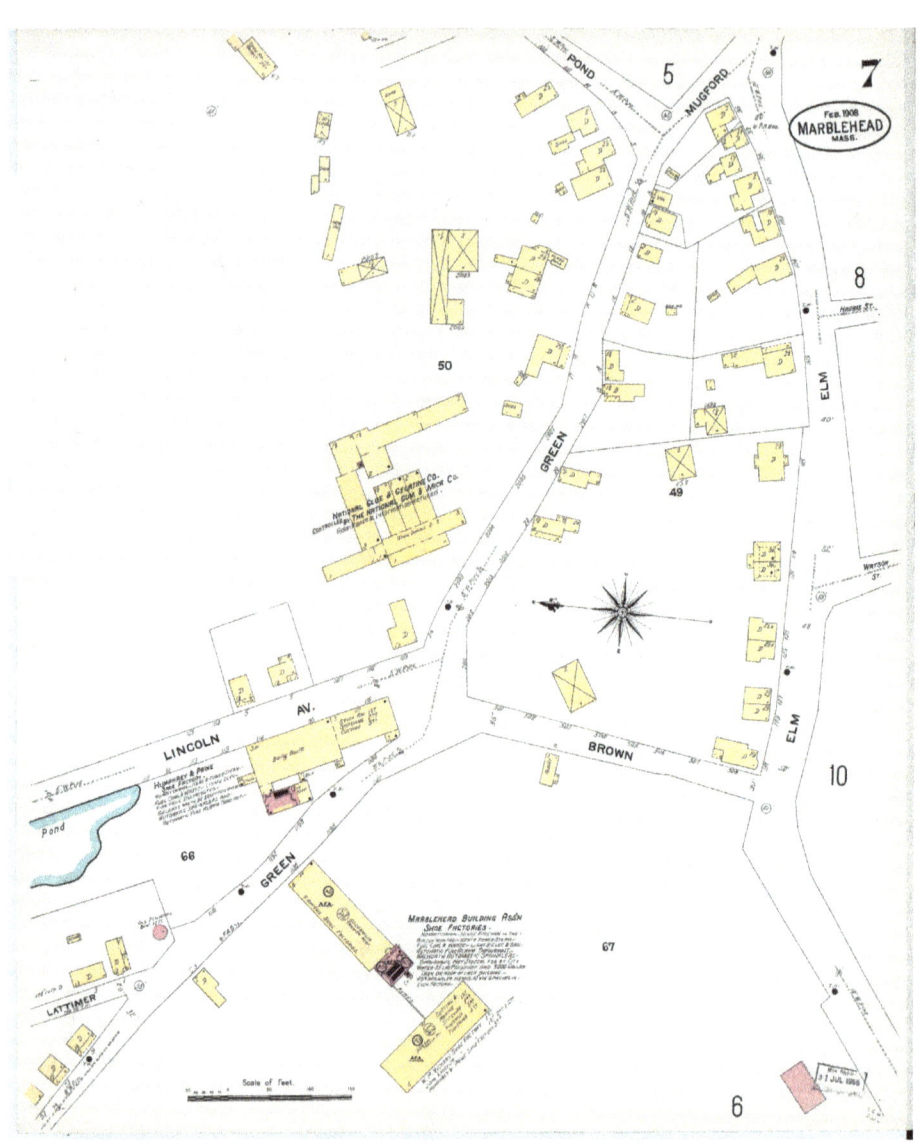

Fort Glover Road, now Bubier Road, from top of hill looking towards Atlantic Ave. November 10, 1914.

Birthday party for Dorothy Litchman in the backyard at 10 High Street on July 15, 1916. Kids playing "Ring Around a Rosey".

Playing "London Bridge"

Mary Pickford on Marblehead Neck, while filming the movie "Pride of the Clan" on November 6, 1916.

Richard Tutt Jr, Age 10 months, 1894

The ferry sign on Front Street near Ferry Lane in 1938.

Ed Farrell (left) and Wormstead (right), Civil War Veteran with cannon beside the Lee Mansion on Washington Street.

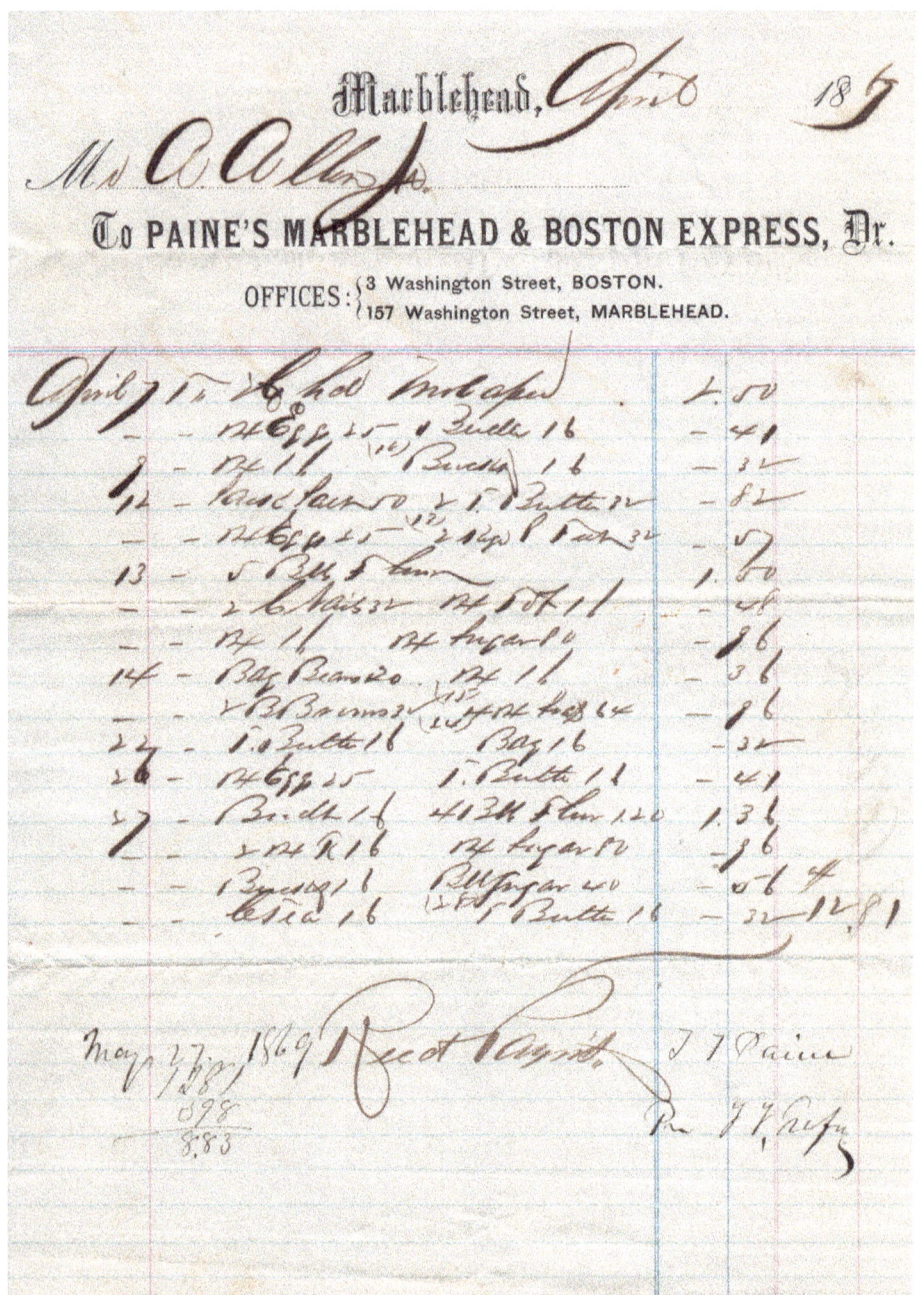

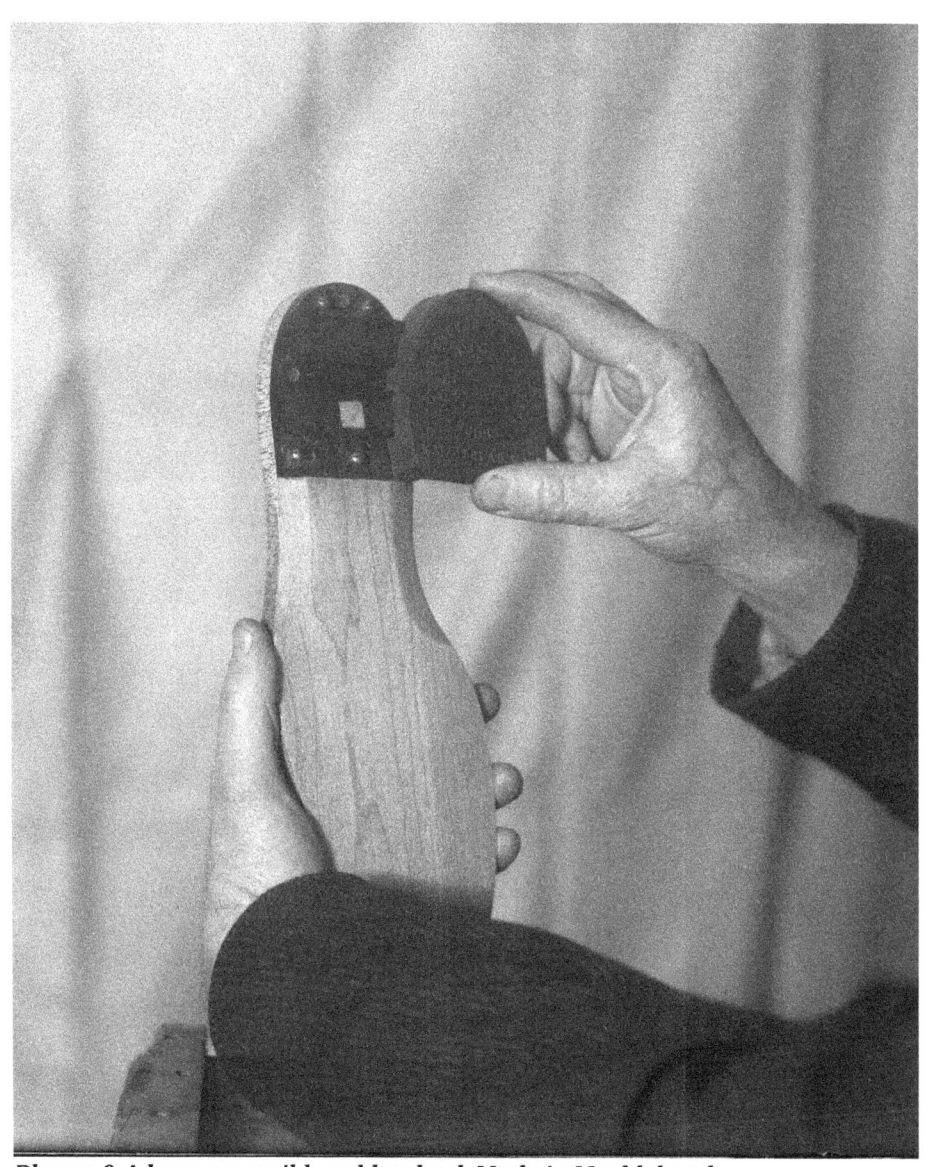

Blaney & Adams reversible rubber heel. Made in Marblehead.

Martha and Elizabeth Lord beside the Lee Mansion

State Street, 2023

Gatchell Farm House, occupied by Jim Goss for 22 years, located near Gatchell's Pit. In 1916, this house was moved to a lot on Baldwin Road.

Girls on bikes on State Street in 1898

The Sea Gull at 146 Washington Street in 1988

Tien's on School Street in 1988

Horsefeathers at 259 Washington Street in 1988

Washington Street Bar and Grill, 259 Washington Street in 1991

Ateller and RSVP Thelma 51 Atlantic Avenue in 1986

Lynn Marine Supply on Front Street in 1985

The India Star, from Salem, and the Marblehead ferry Delta, sighseeing trips on a foggy day in 1979.

Little Harbor in 1988

The Landing in 1988

Cassidy Real Estate, One Essex Street in 1988

Rockmere Hotel July 5, 1964. It was empty, at the time, and was torn down in 1965.

The King's Rook, 12 State Street in 1986.

Anchor Fuel and Village Rug on Bessom Street in 1969

Bus Stop store in 1988

Claire House in Town House Square in 1985

Skating on Marblehead Harbor in 1979

State Street in 2023

Glover's Regiment firing cannon at Fort Sewall in 2023

F/V Karen B, Steve Bird and crew in 1978

Information Booth on Pleasant Street in 1991

1997

1997

Country Home, Marine Art of Marblehead, on Washington Street in 1988

6-17-1987

7-19-1981

Manford L Porter in 1979

Frozen harbor in 1979.

1986

Maddies Sail Loft in 1990

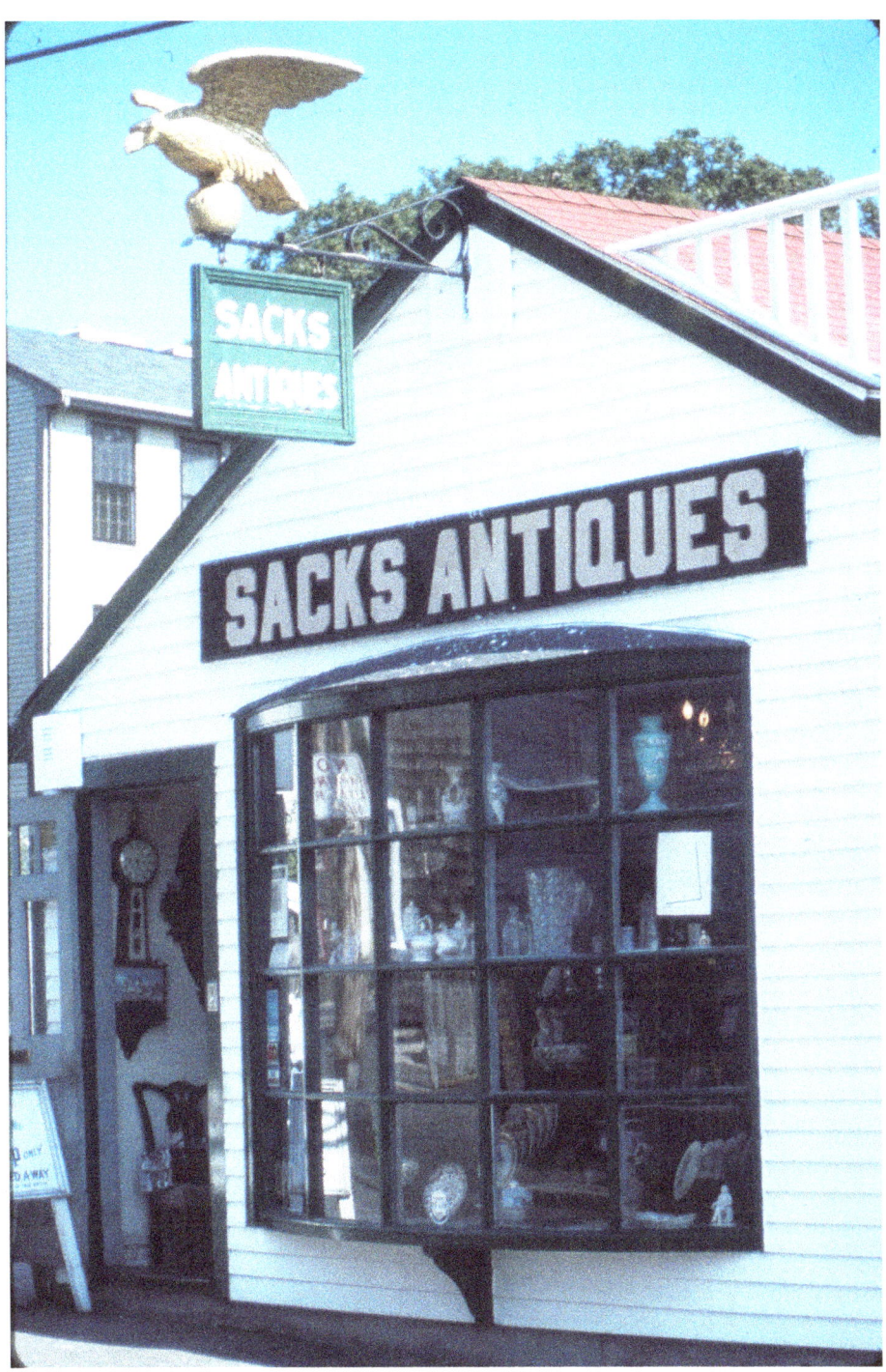
Sack's Antiques in 1988

Bette Hunt and Fred Bauer at Glover's Regiment Encampment at Fort Sewall in July 1994

Front Street during the USS Constitution visit in 1997

Marblehead Kite Company in 1988

The Five Corners Deli in 1991

Front Street in front of The Barnacle on June 9, 1979.

Ken Herwitz painting at the State Street landing

Rosalie's restaurant on Sewall Street in 1988

Frank Osborne in the Liquor Store at Osborne's Store on the corner of School Street and Pleasant Street

Dill's Restaurant

Linc Hawkes with his bull on State Street on Election Day in 1982

Dan Dixey driving Marblehead Health Department trash packer in 1978 at garage on Tower Way

Acknowledgments

The book would not have been possible without advice from Sue Dixey.

A partial list of those that have contributed or helped in some way over the years leading up to this book: My Family, all of the Marblehead lobstermen, Joanne Goodwin, Gayle Griffiths Fraser, Roger Tuveson, Dana Brown, Robb Kipp, Charlie Maurais, Hooper Goodwin, Bobbi Livingston Amirault, Bruce Bowman, Judy Rawding, Brenda Till Dumais, Barb Perry, Bill & Irene Conly, Wayne Attridge, Jack Attridge, Marge Gallo Armstrong, Andrea Tucker Merrifield, Patty Pederson, Bill Glass, Will Williams, Lauren McCormick, Steve Hutchins, Bette Hunt, Gail Anderson, Dave Crowley, Gene Arnould, Bill Frost, Jason Gilliland, Don Doliber, Ben Rhodes, Webb & Sharon Russell, Jimmy Davenport, Paulette Brophy, Jan Frost, George Shube, John Kelley, Chip Percy, Stephen Hall, Joan Cutler, Brad Smith, Judy Anderson, Dave Howells, Rick Ashley, Barry Dixey, Cliff Smith, Ricky Bartlett, Tanya Braganti, Julie Matuschak, Cynthia Andrews VanVoorhis, Sue Coffey, Tom Ball, Lisa Piper, Lisa Welch McCarthy, Dana Tufts, Michael Lafayette, Joyce St. Pierre Preble, Pat Lausier, George Carruth, Harold Hansen, David and Terri Hutchinson, Vinny McGrath, Ann Oswald, Doug Redfield, Phil Leahy, Curt Havens, Colleen Galvin and Luisa Capasso. The Forever Marbleheaders group, The Shinn Family, The Dixey Family, The Grader Family, The Kaplan Family, The LeBlanc Family, The Helen Dixey Doane family, The Family of John "Harpo" Belanger, Marblehead Museum, Town of Marblehead, and many consultations with Maureen Graves Anderson and Denise Alkonis Wolff. Last but not least, my regular coffee meetings with Wayne Attridge in Maine and Marblehead.

And will never forget: Vincent Dixey, John Griffiths, Warren Perry, Bill Goodwin, Ted Peach, Harry Wilkinson, Ben Woodfin, Louise Martin Cutler, Ben Chadwick, Harry Christensen, Chet Sawtell, Bert Symonds, Chris Brown, Marion Gosling, Bowd Osborne, Ray Cole,

Dave Moynihan, Hooper Cutler, Michael Clough, Anne Penni, and Larry Hardwick.

Sources used:
New England's Plantation with the Sea Journal, Reverend Francis Higginson
Letters from New England to England by Francis Higginson
History of Salem, Massachusetts, Vol I, II, III, Sidney Perley, 1924
The Indian Land Titles of Essex County, Massachusetts, Sidney Perley, 1912
History and Traditions of Marblehead, Samuel Roads Jr., 1880
The Founding of Marblehead, Thomas E. Gray, 1984
Dixey Family Letters, Deeds, Wills, and Other Documents
Historical Outline of the Marblehead Police Department by Donald Doliber Sr.
Glover's Marblehead Regiment, In the War of the Revolution, F.A. Gardner, M.D.
Southern Essex District Registry of Deeds, https://salemdeeds.com
Abbot Public Library, Community History Archive, http://marbleheadpl.advantage-preservation.com

Index

A

Benjamin Abbot 13
Abbot Hall 12, 13, 55, 70, 137
Abby Mays 13
Adams 14, 33, 55, 76, 77, 85, 102, 153
Adams House 14, 85, 102
Allerton 11, 12, 15, 52, 81
Arnould Gallery 16

B

Bank Square 17, 18, 87, 88, 97, 139
Barnacle 61, 85, 182
Barnard Hawkes Court v, 18
Bartlett 35, 37, 76, 77, 138, 188
Bartol 7, 65, 77
Bassett 14, 18, 67, 68
Beacon Restaurant 63
Bide-A-Wee 23, 60, 89
Blackler 8, 10, 18, 36
Bowden 10, 23, 37, 40, 55
Bridgeo 8, 10
Broughton 18, 19, 21, 36, 37, 55, 57, 61
Brown's Bakery 61, 89
Burgess 22, 23, 80, 83

C

Cash 18, 37
Caswell 10, 37, 49, 55, 77
CBYC 23
Chadwick 8, 10, 47, 188
Chamberlain 21, 106
Chapman 13, 77, 83, 133, 141
Children's Island 45, 46
Christmas Walk 23, 24
Churches 24
Churn 26
Clifton 25, 26, 27, 44, 55, 59, 66, 123, 141
Cloon 101
Coffin 66
Colbert 39, 40

Cook's Corner 27
Cotter 13
Craddock 15
Curtis 10, 22, 77

D

Damon Tucker's 28, 102
Devereux 7, 10, 19, 28, 29, 30, 31, 34, 37, 38, 39, 51, 55, 59, 65, 70, 73, 121, 123
Dill's 61, 63, 186
Dixey i, ii, iii, 8, 10, 15, 16, 17, 18, 32, 37, 38, 54, 55, 56, 57, 60, 65, 79, 116, 187, 188, 189
Doane 125, 188
Dodd 8, 10
Doliber 7, 10, 37, 55, 57, 76, 77, 78, 188, 189
Down Bucket 31
Driftwood 62, 143

E

Eustis 97

F

Farrell 151
Flynnie's 63
Jeff Flynn 63
Fort Beach 19, 71, 94
Fort Sewall 14, 34, 35, 71, 94, 102, 113, 128, 130, 165, 178
Foss 14, 57, 78
Franklin Street 7, 14, 24, 32, 33, 51, 105, 106, 135
Freeto 9, 76
Frost 8, 9, 33, 36, 37, 55, 62, 109, 188

G

Gale 7, 8, 34, 49, 53, 70
Gerry 5 54, 106, 108
Gerry Island 46, 121
Gilbert 10, 110
Gilbert and Cole 110
Girdler 10, 37

Glover 10, 11, 20, 32, 35, 36, 37, 38, 44, 61, 66, 127, 145, 165, 178, 189
Glover's Regiment 37, 165, 178
Goldthwait 19, 30, 33
Grand Banks 8
Graves 9, 10, 30, 37, 38, 65, 76, 79, 127, 188
Great Race 38, 39
Gregory 11, 12, 13, 25, 35, 44, 57, 62, 100
Grocers 39, 47
Gun House 41, 101

H

Hammond 96, 106
Havens 63, 79, 188
Hawkes v, 18, 19, 49, 53, 55, 186
Headers i, 41, 64, 72, 79
Hector's Pup 99
Herreshoff 42
Francis Higginson 7, 189
Homan 10, 18, 19, 37, 55, 65
Hood 21
Hooper 8, 10, 18, 32, 37, 43, 47, 55, 60, 65, 77, 81, 87, 118, 137, 188, 189
Hotels 43
House of Pizza 13
Humphrey 10, 12, 21, 26, 37, 66, 67, 69, 72
Hutchie's 45
Hutchinson 45, 188

I

Ireson 30, 33, 34, 77

J

Jacob Marley's 63
Jermyn 31, 32
Joe Frogger 20, 46
Johnson 7, 15, 76

K

King's Rook 47, 162

L

Landing Restaurant 62
Lead Mill 47, 48, 108
Lee Mansion 18, 35, 48, 59, 91, 151, 154
Lemmon 57, 126
Litchman 35, 58, 87, 120, 146
Lyceum 43, 49

M

MacDonald's Restaurant 61
Maddie's 35, 38, 61, 114
Manataug Bottling 49
Marblehead Mercantile 50
Marblehead Museum 48, 50, 188
Marblehead Pottery 51, 121
Marblehead Supermarket 40
Martin 10, 13, 37, 43, 51, 55, 77, 79, 92, 101, 106, 188
Mary Alley 30, 42, 51, 52
Mason 35, 37, 83, 141
Ma Toft's 49
Maverick 7, 15, 28, 46, 52
McClain 52
McNulty 17, 77, 78
Merritt 7, 36
Mino's 36, 53
Molly Waldo 62
Monuments 53
Mugford 8, 21, 26, 32, 40, 41, 53, 56, 86

N

National Grand Bank 18, 49, 87, 137, 139
Naugus Head vi, 15, 32, 34, 35, 45, 55, 111, 112
Neighborhoods 55
Nicholson Hill v, 56

O

Old Burial Hill 8, 24, 35, 53, 75, 76, 83, 90
Old Town 19, 24, 55, 56, 57, 60, 126
Old Town House 19, 56, 57, 126
Orne 21, 35, 37, 46, 57, 60, 84, 90
Osborne 40, 91, 133, 185, 188

P

Peach vi, 7, 12, 23, 37, 55, 57, 77, 113, 127, 188
Peach's Point vi, 57, 57–81
Pedrick 8, 9, 10, 37, 65, 106
Penni's 41
Percy 63, 188
Pickett 32, 37, 105
Pitman 7, 10, 28, 57
Pool Halls 58
Poorhouses 58
Porter 19, 173
Powder House 59

R

Rechabite 11, 12, 58
Redd 7, 8, 19, 60, 81, 99, 108
Redd's Pond 8, 19, 60, 81, 99, 108
Rip Tide 61, 64
Riverhead 19
Roads 10, 26, 30, 55, 64, 65, 66, 189
Rockmere 44, 57, 81, 136, 162
Rodgers 55, 100
Rosalie's 62, 184
Roundy 13, 77

S

Sadie's 64
Saltwater Bookstore 64
Schoolhouses 64
Seaside Park 35, 42, 67, 133
Sebastian Miniatures 67
Sewall 11, 14, 18, 34, 35, 48, 62, 65, 68, 71, 94, 102, 113, 120, 128, 129, 130, 165, 178, 184
Shube 39, 40, 78, 188

Sneakers Restaurant 63
Sorosis Farm 69, 118, 139
Stacey 10, 37, 68, 69, 85, 106
Standley 8, 10, 77
Stone 10, 14, 18, 55, 106
Storms 70
Submarine Base 51

T

Tent's 57, 67, 72
Three Cod Tavern 61, 63
Timmie's 73
Tony's Pizza 62
Trasher 10
Trefry 10, 37
Tucker 28, 31, 37, 47, 57, 79, 102, 188
Tutt 148

U

USS Constitution 74, 75, 179

V

Village Plaza 62, 73, 75, 95

W

Wars 76
Warwick 17, 39, 60, 63, 78, 79
Wharfs 79
Whip 79, 143
Williams 37, 95, 188
William Walton 24, 75, 76
Winslow's 80
Woodfin 11, 44, 54, 55, 69, 77, 188
Wormstead 11, 69, 77, 87, 151

Y

Yacht Club 22, 23, 41, 44, 60, 80, 81, 126
YMCA 17, 43, 46, 78, 81

www.ingramcontent.com/pod-product-compliance
Lightning Source LLC
Chambersburg PA
CBHW040107100526
44584CB00029BA/3891